D0351356

# simple japanese

## with east|west flavours

Silla Bjerrum

Photography by Lars Ranek

Quadrille

# contents

# introduction

I returned to London in the early nineties to finish my Bachelor's degree from Copenhagen University as a correspondent student while enjoying the London club scene. To support myself I took a job as a kitchen hand at a friend of a friend's restaurant, Nippon Tuk. This was a small, eccentric place in Chelsea run by Jeremy Rose and Michael Heycock. Michael taught me the basic skills of sushi-making whereas Jeremy taught me about life. I spent four years at Nippon Tuk, picking up techniques and lots of helpful routine, as well as visiting Japan for short periods to work in restaurants serving classical Japanese cuisine and tasting the real deal at source.

During this time I developed a deep fascination not only with Japan's food, but also its culture and people. Initially I wanted to master sushi skills in the traditional way (ie, patiently improving my sushi rice, fine-tuning my knife skills and producing maki and nigiri sushi as close as possible to the authentic original). In 1996 I did a Master of Arts at Goldsmith's College and planned a career in publishing. However the sushi market in London was growing fast and the demand for sushi makers was high. I decided to accept that my fate and my talent was with Japanese food.

I went to work for Birley's in Canary Wharf, hand-producing an outrageous number of lunch boxes Monday to Friday. However repetitive I found making the same three lunch boxes day-in and day-out, it proved an essential experience. It gave me an opportunity to learn more about good routines and the serious side of running a kitchen successfully – things like margin control, staff levels, hygiene, health and safety and so on. The sushi was very popular, pushing me to a five o'clock morning start on a dark industrial estate in Battersea. After two years of this I threw in the towel to work in a more 'human' environment.

Jeremy Rose and I again joined forces as business partners and, together with our financial backers, started Feng Sushi in the summer of 1999. Our first outlet was on Fulham Road; a small local branch with a faithful clientele. During the last seven years we have opened another five branches throughout London, offering a very successful delivery service. From its inception, Feng Sushi has been built on two simple principles: impeccably sourced, quality food made and sold by a young, international, well-trained team.

Starting a small business has been a hands-on experience and provided a steep learning curve. Our strength has been Jeremy's flair for clever locations, good front-of-house management, and my time in the kitchen ensuring that the team understands the product. The rest we picked up as we went along with experiences both hilarious and stressful. Throughout this time Jeremy and I have stuck to two mottos: 'if our fish was any fresher we would have to slap it', and 'you are only as good as your supplier'.

Not being a classically trained chef has been at times difficult: sometimes you feel you lack the lingo and the mannerisms. But never forget that the air of confidence around a good chef often comes from hours spent in the kitchen paying attention to details, not necessarily from catering colleges. In my opinion the growing breed of self-taught 'cooks' brings fresh air to the restaurant scene, and is a healthy alternative to this constant babble from top chefs about who is and who is not a 'real' chef.

My approach to food is based on my eating experiences – past, present and future – plus reading a lot of cookbooks and magazines. The procedure is very simple: 'This tastes or sounds delicious, I wonder if it would work with this...?' And from there it is trial and error. I believe most dishes need to be cooked over and over again before achieving the desired result.

I am also from a large family of foodies. Every seasonal or social event is celebrated with a big feast of new, fashionable cooking. For us this is a serious business: if you invite people around it is to impress and this can be a daunting experience for new members of the family or friends. However, good and constructive criticism is valuable at times. With this background I have always been eager to try new things, in particular when visiting new places or people with a different background to mine.

I like to fuse sushi with Scandinavian and European flavours as it is the food I grew up with and know well. Therefore the sushi and Japanese food in this book is a mixture of classic Japanese dishes and simple tasty new ones with a foreign accent – such as gravadlax

nigiri, which is traditional Scandinavian cured salmon made with Thai herbs instead of dill and served on sushi rice with an Asian-style pesto. Another popular fusion dish is Japanese-style fish and chips with rémoulade, a Japanese interpretation of the traditional British favourite with a Danish detour provided by the rémoulade dipping sauce.

The idea for this book came from my experience training chefs in-house and at the sushi classes I have been running for the general public, businesses and charities since spring 2003. I realised that many of our customers were interested in learning some basic techniques for making their own sushi at home. My strong belief is that anyone willing to learn can be taught how to make Japanese food.

There are two issues about which I am militant: good sourcing of fresh fish (for more on this see pages 10-13) and cooking sushi rice correctly. The former is a given, but the latter is often ignored. Remember: good sushi relies 50 per cent on perfectly cooked sushi rice, so you need to follow the instructions on pages 14-15 with precision, and use proper sushi rice, which is now widely available.

Patience and persistence can make a decent sushi cook of most people and with this knowledge I felt that it would be exiting to put some of my favourite recipes in book form. Japanese cooking requires skill, but once you have mastered a small set of basic techniques the world really is your oyster.

**Silla Bjerrum**

# the starter kit

You need very few tools to make sushi: a bamboo rolling mat for making rolls and a nigiri mould for shaping rice blocks. These are available in most Asian stores. A mandolin cuts julienne of vegetables quickly and easily. It is also worth investing in a couple of Japanese knives. The ones shown here are not expensive, but any good chef's knife and a filleting knife will do. A tamago pan is essential for making rolled Japanese omelettes. Season it by gently simmering 100g salt in a few inches of vegetable oil for ten minutes, cool it and discard the oil and the pan will last you for decades.

The basic ingrdients for sushi are widely available. They are also good store cupboard items (a packet of nori lasts forever unopened) so you can keep them for whenever you feel inspired. Buying sushi vinegar instead of making your own minimises the number of items you need. Finally, make sure you buy proper sushi rice (a short-grained round, polished variety). A mid-priced brand will give excellent results but choose one grown in the hemisphere in which you live because the rice suffers from the high humidity when crossing the equator.

Clockwise from the bottom left: chopping board, bamboo rolling mat, deba knife, sashimi knife, mandolin, nigiri mould, acidulated water, sesame oil, soy sauce, nori, dashi powder, wasabi, pickled ginger, black and white toasted sesame seeds, sushi rice.

# fishstory fish for sashimi, sushi and other japanese dishes

I have developed a habit of judging a place and its people by its fish. It may not be a totally fair approach from a sociological perspective, but at least it will get me up early to seek out the local fish market. I have visited markets in small fishing communities with a few boats and a smokehouse, massive frozen warehouses full of imported goods, commercial markets with separate sections for the trade and the public, and all of very different standards.

The one I will always love most is Tsukiji in Tokyo. The first time I went to Tsukiji I was so impressed I went back three times during my trip. Now whenever I go to Tokyo I go there most mornings because it is the most fascinating commercial fish market in the world. Set by Tokyo bay, it has the sea behind it and the city in front. The standard of hygiene is high and I was surprised not to find the sharp smell often associated with fish trading. There I learned the most important lesson: fresh fish does not smell fishy, it smells of the sea, fresh and salty.

Most Tokyo tour guides recommend visiting Tsukiji to see the tuna auction first thing in the morning. This is when the pricy imported bluefin tuna is sold to stallholders in the market and then on to the restaurant trade. However if you miss this, there is

still plenty to satisfy all your senses. The market at first seems chaotic, with people rushing around, traders shouting prices and boxes of fish stacked high everywhere. You have to negotiate a maze of little paths, being careful not to get run over by a trader ruthlessly driving his motorised cart through the market, or standing too close to someone nonchalantly using a chainsaw to cut down a frozen bluefin tuna. There are big stalls offering bright red tuna in glass display cases, as though they were the crown jewels. Then there are stalls specialising in every fish known to Japanese cuisine: one selling sea urchin, another salmon eggs, a third offering mainly squid and octopus, and so on.

On the outskirts of the market there are more opportunities for shopping: greengrocers, cookbook stands, utensil shops, a retailer selling shaved ice, and small sushi bars serving the freshest sushi imaginable. There is an amazing tamago shop that does nothing other than make Japanese omelettes all day: a line of five to six tamago chefs work together, mass-producing beautiful handmade omelettes for the sushi bars in town.

Tsukiji has taught me a lot of what I expect of the fish I buy for my restaurants in London. For sashimi and sushi, most of the fish is eaten raw and therefore the quality and freshness is imperative. To ensure good taste, presentation and food safety, there are some key points to follow:

● Buy your fish from a highly regarded fishmonger or fish market, preferably a shop with which you have some history, or which has been recommended by someone who cares about good quality ingredients.
● Be aware that fish sold on Mondays is often Saturday's stock, as most shops close on Sundays.
● Always make your fishmonger aware that you

intend to serve the fish raw, and ask for 'sashimi-grade' fish, which also indicates that it is going to be eaten raw.
● Very few supermarkets sell sashimi-grade fish. Even though the fish will be perfectly all right to eat cooked, it may not be good enough to consume raw.
● Always buy fish on the same day you want to use it, and put it straight in the fridge when you get home.

In addition, you should follow these basic rules:
● When buying whole fish always ask for it scaled, gutted and cleaned. It saves you the dirty work and you are minimising the risk of cross-contamination in your own kitchen.
● When buying whole fish look for clear eyes and bright red, spongy and odour-free gills.
● When buying filleted fish choose odour-free, firm-textured fillets that still have a natural sheen.
● When buying a loin of fish, ensure that it is cut from the middle of the fish as the tail piece often has a lot of tissue that is of little use.
● A loin should also look fresh and be free of dark patches or dryness.

It is worth taking some interest in how, and from where, the fish we eat arrives. The key issues are fishing methods, handling, distance and transportation. In general, line-caught fish is better than net-caught, providing that the lines are in the water for a minimum of time. The main problem with net-caught fish is the by-catch: sometimes 50 per cent of the fish pulled is dropped back dead into the sea, killed for no purpose. Furthermore, some fish will be damaged by the sheer weight of the nets when they are pulled up from the water.

Fish caught by large commercial trawlers are sometimes fished with so little consideration for fish stocks and the environment that the nets are dragged deeper and deeper, taking everything in their wake, like an evil Godzilla of the sea. I prefer small off-shore day boats, which go to sea for a few days and fish in sustainable waters. With good handling of the fish on board, the fish is fresher, arrives intact and fetches a better price at the market.

In serving fish every day in our restaurants, I take responsibility for including and promoting locally caught fish wherever possible, to save on air miles. We have got so used to a world of mass-produced, globally transported food that we all expect to be able to eat everything and anything year-round. However the pressure on suppliers and fishermen to get it right can only come from the consumer, whether it is buying fish for home cooking or going out for a meal.

I am a great advocate of sustainable (that is: ecologically friendly) fish farming. Farmed fish can be successful if the producers consider the welfare of the animals and the environment. The salmon farming industry has been under pressure for a number of years to improve its ways. The good initiatives are few and far between, but there are some good products on the market. I choose farmed salmon for various reasons. A good quality farmed salmon is safer to eat raw than a fish caught in the wild as the risk of parasites and fish worm is minimal. Salmon farmed correctly will avoid dioxins in the flesh by using fishmeal made from fish caught in unpolluted waters. Furthermore, giving the salmon plenty of room in their pens (less than one per cent fish to 99 per cent water) will make the fish fit and happy. They not only taste better and have a firmer texture than other farmed fish, they are leaner, and lean fish contain fewer toxins and dioxins because these substances are stored in the fat tissue.

For the last four years I have been fortunate to be using salmon from Loch Duart, a company based at the northwest tip of the Scottish mainland. Loch Duart produces salmon to very high standards and has a fallow system in place for their four farms, so that every year one farm is taken out of production to give the sea bed time to recover from any impact the farming may have had. Furthermore, they do not use chemicals on their pen nets. Instead the salmon are moved to an empty pen every six weeks, and the nets are pulled up to let the algae dry naturally in the sun and wind. The algae are a good source of minerals for the fish. Loch Duart salmon is a little dearer than other farmed salmon, but the difference in taste and texture is outstanding. Hopefully more and more restaurants will demand salmon of this type and quality, and subsequently put pressure on the whole industry to change.

In the case of tuna, it is difficult not to consume air miles. Tuna for the sushi trade in Europe comes mostly from Sri Lanka or the Maldives. As the popularity of sushi has grown worldwide over the past 20 years, tuna fishing has also been intensified. The annual catch is now approximately 1.2 million tons. Japan is catching 350,000 tons of tuna around Japan itself, and importing 250,000 tons annually, therefore taking 50 percent of the global tuna catch.

There are seven known species of tuna, however for sushi the most popular are bluefin, 1000 bluefin, yellowfin and bigeye. The bigeye has a very high fat content and therefore, in one sense, is perfect for sushi. However the flesh loses its colour as soon as it is exposed to air and the fish should be eaten straight after it has been pulled out of the water – making it unsuitable for the European market. Often bigeye is vacuum-packed as soon as it is landed on deck, making it even less suitable to eat raw.

There are two cuts of bluefin very popular on the Japanese market. Most in demand is the belly flap or toro. Toro looks almost like marbled beef and has a pink hue compared to the leaner cut called maguro that comes from the top loin of the fish. Fishing for tuna is a highly technical operation and most tuna for the Japanese market is fished from large boats. The tuna is line-caught and once landed on deck is gutted, bled and then graded. The best fish are nitrogen-frozen as these will fetch the highest price when sold on. This is a very good method of preservation as it helps to kill any bacteria growth in the flesh of the fish. So popular is bluefin tuna in Japan that 80 per cent of the global catch ends up there. Bluefin tuna is only seen on the European market during the summer months when they swim with the Gulf Stream into the Mediterranean Sea.

Unfortunately, due to its high popularity and extreme over-fishing, bluefin tuna is in serious danger of extinction. Some tuna is now being farmed in Croatia, Australia and Italy. Young tuna are taken from the wild and then reared in large fenced areas along the seashore. The problem with this method is that breeding stock is being taken out of the wild stock, which can have consequences for the future population. Around the world various schemes have been devised to help preserve the bluefin tuna. However, as there is still concern about stocks of this species, I prefer using yellowfin tuna.

Mainly from an ecological point of view, but also from a financial and practical standpoint, there are many reasons to favour yellowfin tuna. It is difficult for us to guarantee a stable supply of bluefin as the best quality fish fetch a better price on the Japanese market. Bluefin is often very expensive and the loin, with its highly desirable toro, provides little meat for lean tuna dishes.

Most yellowfin on the European market is from Sri Lanka or the Maldives. The tuna is line-caught and once landed on deck is gutted, bled and kept in an ice slush to cool it down. All tuna prefer warm waters of 17-27°C, however when killed there is a risk of histamine poisoning if they are kept above 5°C, and to some people this can be deadly. All tuna for sushi consumption is checked for safe levels of histamine.

When buying tuna for Japanese dishes always ask for the middle cut as this will provide the greatest yield. You can buy tuna one day in advance of serving providing you wrap it tightly in kitchen paper and then in cling film; kept like this it will firm up overnight in a similar manner to beef.

Yellowtail, or hamachi, is a common name for amberjack fish, which is an oily variety with light grey coloured flesh and a rich, buttery flavour somewhere between mackerel and tuna. Yellowtail belongs to the same family as tuna, bonito and mackerel. Most yellowtail is imported frozen from Japan or Australia, where they are raised in hatcheries and harvested when they weigh 7-10 kilograms. Although yellowtail is sold in frozen fillets it is suitable for eating raw.

Sea bass is another fish being farmed successfully, particularly in Greece, which has become the market leader. As with salmon, farmed sea bass is safer than wild to eat raw, because there is minimal risk of the parasites and fish worm that are often found in the fish but which normally disappear during cooking. In addition, wild sea bass sometimes feed on a green weed containing high levels of bacteria growth, something that can be easily got rid of during cooking, but not when eaten raw. Sea bass are farmed in round cages just offshore in the clean and calm waters of the Greek islands. A good size sea bass for sushi and sashimi is 600-800 grams.

Mackerel is the most underrated fish in Europe and a pertinent example of the bad handling of fish. Often mackerel, because it usually achieves a low price in the market, is just seen as by-catch of other fish. Obviously if the fish is not treated well it will not look presentable at the fish counter and will end up in the stock pot – something I find unbearable as line-caught, well-handled mackerel is the most beautiful fish. An oily fish, high in healthy Omega 3, it is suitable for inclusion in almost any diet. In Japanese cuisine mackerel tends to be pickled or grilled, as this is safer than eating it raw. I am particularly fond of mackerel; it is very common to see a smokehouse by each harbour along the Danish coast, which brings back memories of excellent sailing trips with my father. In Britain, Cornish line-caught mackerel is also excellent and widely available for much of the year. Most comes from the fish market at Newlyn, Penzance, where it is landed by small day boats.

Prawns, especially black tiger prawns, are also popular in Japanese cuisine. In general prawn farms have a very bad reputation, with only a few improving their farming methods in recent years. Ask your fishmonger what he knows about the origin of his tiger prawns. Good quality fresh prawns are often flown in from Nigeria and Madagascar, but this unfortunately consumes many air miles. For acceptable frozen tiger prawns, Malaysia currently has a better reputation than most producing regions and their prawns are transported frozen by sea.

Another delicious ingredient used in this book is the scallop. Hand-diving for scallops is a much gentler method of harvesting these bivalves than trawling. The method was developed in Scotland when the off-shore oil industry was being built. Freelance divers were looking for a way of earning money during the periods when they where not diving for the oil rigs and realised there was a market for hand-dived scallops. Hand-diving has a very low environment impact, because the divers dive the same areas time after time and hand-pick the scallops instead of scraping up everything from the sea bed. Often the divers will keep smaller scallops in underwater cages (a process similar to lobster fishing) until they have grown to a good size. Hand-dived scallops, whether from Dorset or Scotland, are absolutely divine.

# fail-safe sushi rice

This method produces 1.1kg of prepared sushi rice; the quantities can easily be doubled or quadrupled.

1 Put 500g sushi rice in a large mixing bowl.

2 The rice needs to be 'rough' washed four or five times. To do this, fill the bowl with cold water and stir the rice with your hand, but not so vigorously that you break the rice kernels. After each wash tip the water out and start again.

3 After four or five washes the water will be cloudy rather than milky white. Now wash the rice another four times, but each time tip the rice into a sieve to get rid of all the water.

4 Leave the rice to rest for 30 minutes in the sieve, then measure the volume of rice in a jug. To cook it, put the rice in a rice cooker or saucepan. Add enough water to give 110 per cent of the volume of rice. Do not add salt. If using an electric rice cooker, turn it on and when it has finished cooking, leave it to rest for 17 minutes. If cooking the rice in a saucepan, bring it to the boil, cover and let it simmer for 17 minutes, then leave to it stand for 17 minutes.

5 When the rice has rested, empty it into a tray and leave to 'steam off' for about 10 minutes, until it reaches 50°C. It is important not to add sushi vinegar to very hot rice or the humidity will cause the grains to collapse.

6 Position a portable fan so that it blows cold air directly on to the rice. Sprinkle 65ml sushi vinegar over the rice and incorporate it by making diagonal strokes across the rice with a spatula. Leave the rice under the fan for about 10 minutes, until it cools to room temperature, or 24-28°C. The rice is now ready to use. If necessary, you can store it up to four hours at room temperature, but do not chill it.

# sashimi

Sashimi is the freshest and best quality fish served raw. The cutting technique is vital, because the cut *is* the cooking. Everything must be sliced on the bias, so that you cut through the fibres to make the fish tender. Patience and practice can make any novice a sashimi master. All the recipes in this chapter are for four people, assuming you are serving them in combination with another dish, or as a starter course.

Yellowtail sashimi verde

# cutting sides of large fish

In these pictures we are working with a whole side of salmon, however you would use the same technique for sides of other large round fish such as yellowtail.

1. Divide the side of salmon into three by cutting along the line of the spine, then crossways at the tail end. Set aside the tail end (you can freeze it or poach it) for use in other dishes. The thicker, rectangular fillet (on the left hand side of the picture opposite) is for sashimi, the flatter, more triangular fillet (on the right) is for nigiri.

2. Run your hands gently along the sashimi fillet to stretch it. Use a knife to trim off any brown meat as thinly as possible.

3. Trim the sashimi fillet by $1/2$-1cm on each side to give a neat rectangular block. Save the trimmings and the brown meat for use in other cooking.

4. When cutting the fish into sashimi pieces you want to slice it across the bias. This means cutting it diagonally along the fillet while at the same time cutting it an angle vertically, always working across the white lines of the flesh. Typically a 45-degree angle is required, but as the lines in the fish vary you may have to reposition the knife periodically so that you keep cutting across the white lines.

5. For nigiri, take the nigiri portion of the side of fish and cut it into blocks of around 6cm. Take the first piece and turn it so that the brown meat is closest to the board. Carefully trim off the brown meat by slicing under the fish as close to the surface of the board as you can.

6. Slice the trimmed block into nigiri pieces across the bias, cutting diagonally with the knife at a 45-degree angle.

# classic salmon sashimi

serves ● ● ● ●

400g Mooli Salad  (see page 45)
400g salmon sashimi block
100g mixed baby salad leaves

**to serve**
wasabi, pickled ginger and soy sauce

First make the mooli salad using the recipe on page 45 and place in the fridge. Trim the salmon block on each side, saving the off-cuts for another dish. Cut 20 pieces of fish sashimi-style (see page 19), slicing along the bias.

Arrange the salad leaves on serving plates and top with the mooli salad. Place five pieces of fish on each plate and serve with wasabi, pickled ginger and soy sauce on the side.

# salmon tartar with spring onions, yuzu tobiko and feng mayo

serves ● ● ● ●

200g Mooli Salad (see page 45)
2 tablespoons Feng Mayo (see page 44)
1 cucumber
320g salmon sashimi block
4 spring onions, green tops only, finely chopped
1 tablespoon yuzu juice
1 tablespoon ponzu sauce
freshly ground black pepper
4 tablespoons yuzu tobiko
a few chives to garnish

**to serve**
wasabi, pickled ginger and soy sauce

Make a half quantity of the mooli salad on page 45, then prepare the Feng Mayo as described on page 44. Peel the cucumber lengthways in long strips, keeping just the skin to use in this recipe – save the flesh for another dish. Cut the salmon into small dice, about $1/2$cm square.

In a mixing bowl, combine the mayo, spring onions, yuzu juice and ponzu sauce, then stir in the salmon and some freshly ground black pepper. Set aside for 4 minutes to let the acid in the citrus 'cook' the salmon. Then transfer the mixture to a sieve to remove the excess liquid and ensure the fish does not overcook. Gently stir in the yuzu tobiko.

Arrange the mooli salad on serving plates. Twirl the cucumber strips to look like a bird's nest and place them on top. Spoon on the salmon tartar (you could shape it using a rice triangle mould, if desired). Garnish with the chives and serve with wasabi, pickled ginger and soy sauce.

# yellowtail sashimi verde

serves ● ● ● ●

As most yellowtail is imported frozen, you will need to defrost it in the fridge overnight. Rinse the fish under a running tap and pat dry with kitchen paper before filleting. If yellowtail is not available, you can substitute tuna, salmon or sea bass.

400g Mooli Salad (see page 45)
320-400g yellowtail sashimi block
about 10g chives
about 40g basil sprigs
50g rocket leaves
1 punnet shiso cress

**for the dipping sauce**
50ml Feng Pesto (see page 44)
2 tablespoons ponzu sauce
1 tablespoon honey
2 teaspoons soy sauce

**to serve**
wasabi, pickled ginger and soy sauce

First make the mooli salad using the method on page 45 and place in the fridge to crisp.

To make the dipping sauce, prepare the Feng Pesto if you have not already done so (see page 44), then take a 50ml portion of it and mix with the ponzu sauce, honey and soy sauce. Place in a squeeze bottle ready to dress the sashimi.

Drain the mooli salad and arrange it on serving plates. Cut the fish into 20 sashimi-style pieces and arrange five slices of fish on top of each portion of mooli salad.

Cut the chives into pieces about 10cm long and arrange them rustically on top of the sashimi.

Lay the basil leaves on the work surface so that they are just overlapping. Place the rocket in a line down the middle and roll the herbs up tight like a big cigar. Slice the roll very finely on the diagonal and arrange the basil and rocket on top of the chives. Garnish with shiso leaves.

Drizzle a little dipping sauce over each portion of sashimi and serve the rest on the side with the wasabi, pickled ginger and soy sauce.

# seared salmon sashimi with black pepper and sesame crust
serves ● ● ● ●

This is a variation on a very popular, simple sashimi. I like to incorporate crunch, heat and flavour by adding a sesame and pepper crust, which also gives it a smug healthy status. The recipe also works perfectly with tuna and/or a somen noodle soup with spinach.

100g mixed white and black sesame
   seeds
2 tablespoons black peppercorns
pinch of sea salt
400g salmon sashimi block
400g Mooli Salad (see page 45)
2 teaspoons sesame oil
2 teaspoons olive oil
100g mixed baby salad leaves

**for the dipping sauce**
20g fresh ginger, finely chopped
1 spring onion, finely chopped
100ml soy sauce
50ml mirin
4 teaspoons runny honey

**to serve**
wasabi and pickled ginger

Crush the sesame seeds, black pepper and salt together using a mortar and pestle, then spread the mixture in a shallow tray. Trim the sashimi block on each side using the instructions on page 18, then cut the block into two pieces. Press the sesame mixture onto fish so that the four long sides of each block are well coated. Put aside to set.

Make the mooli salad according to the instructions on page 45 and place in the fridge to crisp. To make the dipping sauce, combine all the ingredients in a mixing bowl.

In a frying pan, heat the sesame and olive oils together. When spitting hot, fry each block of salmon for no more than 1 minute on each side, just to sear the edge. Remove the fish from the heat and set aside to rest.

Arrange the baby salad leaves and drained mooli salad on four serving plates. Cut each block of salmon into five pieces, slicing on the bias sashimi-style, then place the fish on top of the mooli salad. Serve with the dipping sauce, plus wasabi and pickled ginger.

# upside-down yellowtail sashimi with jalapeño chillies and kimchee dressing

serves • • • •

Japanese food is often paired with Peruvian, Brazilian and Mexican ingredients. It's really no wonder: the passion and fire of South American food is a perfect complement to the controlled nature of Japanese cuisine. I turned this idea 'upside down' to ensure that the yellowtail would not over-marinate. This is the ballerina of sashimi. It takes balance skills to stack this dish, but the result is stunning.

20g dried wakame
small bunch of coriander
50g jalapeño chillies
1 cucumber
1 green-skinned avocado
320-400g yellowtail sashimi block

**for the kimchee dressing**
40ml yuzu juice
4 teaspoons ponzu sauce
4 teaspoons kimchee base

Place the wakame in a bowl, cover with cold water and set aside to rehydrate. Meanwhile, pick 24 perfect leaves from the coriander and set aside on a piece of kitchen paper.

Finely chop the jalapeños, wearing gloves and using a chopping board exclusively for chillies. Cut the cucumber into 20 slices $1/2$ cm thick.

Quarter, stone and peel the avocados. Trim and discard the ends from each quarter, then cut each piece diagonally into 5 slices. Drain the rehydrated wakame in a sieve.

To make the kimchee dressing, mix the yuzu juice, ponzu sauce and kimchee base together in a small bowl and place in a squeeze bottle ready for garnishing.

Prepare the yellowtail following the techniques on page 18. Cut each block diagonally to give 20 sashimi-style pieces.

Arrange a row of five cucumber slices on each serving plate. Top with the yellowtail, then arrange a small cluster of wakame on each stack and sprinkle with the jalapeños. Balance a piece of avocado on top, drizzle with dressing and finish each stack with a coriander leaf.

Tip: if the fish is large, you may get a better yield by splitting the 'sashimi' side straight down the middle, rather than trimming off each side to give a sashimi block. This way you could buy just half a fillet, then use the 'nigiri' side and off cuts for other recipes. However remember that if the fish has been frozen, you must not refreeze the off-cuts.

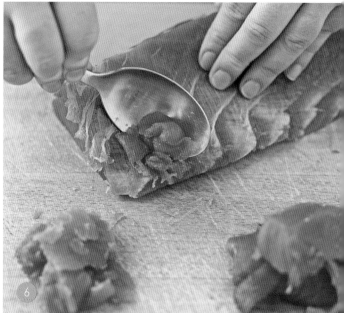

# cutting tuna loin

Mature tuna are exceptionally large specimens, so here we are working with a middle cut of tuna loin.

1. You will see a layer of tissue running through the loin. Turn the fish so that the line of tissue is nearest the board and cut along the loin, following the line of the tissue layer, so that it and the flesh underneath it are detached from the rest of the fillet. Set the off-cut aside.

2. Cut a large slice 3cm thick along the leanest side of the loin. This piece is used for sashimi; the remainder of the loin is used for nigiri. Take the sashimi piece and cut it lengthways to give three long fillets measuring about 3cm wide and 3cm deep. Trim as necessary to give neat rectangular blocks, saving any off-cuts for making maki.

3. Slice each block into sashimi pieces, cutting diagonally along the block and downwards at a 45-degree angle.

4. For nigiri, cut the remaining tuna loin into manageable blocks of about 6cm wide. Turn each block on its side and cut into large slices of 1.5cm.

5. Take each slice of tuna and cut into nigiri pieces, working downwards at a 45 degree angle. The finished nigiri pieces should measure about 6x3cm and just 2mm thick.

6. The off-cuts can quickly be made into tuna mince. To do this, use a metal spoon to carefully scrape the meat away from the layer of white tissue.

# classic tuna sashimi

serves • • • •

400g Mooli Salad (see page 45)
400g yellowfin tuna sashimi block
100g mixed baby salad leaves

**to serve**
wasabi, pickled ginger and soy sauce

Prepare the mooli salad following the instructions on page 45 and place in the fridge to crisp.

Trim the tuna loin into blocks, saving any off-cuts for another dish. Working on the bias, cut the tuna block into 20 sashimi-style pieces (see page 26).

Arrange the salad leaves on serving plates and top with the drained mooli salad. Place five pieces of tuna sashimi on top of each salad and serve with wasabi, pickled ginger and soy sauce on the side.

# tuna tartar with ponzu, spring onions and caviar

serves ● ● ● ●

This is the ideal way to use up leftover tuna and makes a perfect starter.

200g Mooli Salad (see page 45)

2 tablespoons Feng Mayo (see page 44)

1 cucumber

350g sashimi-grade yellowfin tuna

4 spring onions, green tops only, finely chopped

4 tablespoons ponzu sauce

2 tablespoons poppy seeds

50g yuzu tobiko

50g Avruga caviar

freshly ground black pepper

**to serve**

wasabi, pickled ginger and soy sauce

First prepare a half quantity of the mooli salad on page 45 and place in the fridge to crisp. If you have not already done so, make the Feng Mayo as described on page 44.

Peel the cucumber lengthways, keeping the skin and reserving the flesh for use in another recipe.

Mince the tuna, discarding any white tissue. Place in a mixing bowl and add the chopped spring onion tops. Mix in 2 tablespoons of Feng Mayo, plus the ponzu sauce, poppy seeds, yuzu tobiko, Avruga caviar and some freshly ground black pepper and leave to rest for 2 minutes.

Drain the mooli salad and arrange it on four serving plates. Twirl the cucumber strips so that they look like a bird's nest and place on the mooli. Shape the tuna tartar using a mould such as a rice triangle mould, and carefully place each portion on top of the cucumber nest. Serve with wasabi, pickled ginger and soy sauce.

# pici-pici sashimi

serves • • • •

Pici-pici means a friendly slap around the face and this is the ultimate dish for the Feng motto: 'If our fish was any fresher we would have to slap it.'
A mixed sashimi such as this is an opportunity to show off your sourcing and carving skills. Use the best and freshest fish available and as many locally fished species as possible. Here I am using salmon, tuna, mackerel and ikura (salmon eggs), but fish such as sea bass, sea bream, snapper and yellowtail would also work perfectly.

400g Mooli Salad (see page 45)
200g salmon sashimi block
200g yellowfin tuna sashimi block
160g marinated mackerel (see page 33)
120g ikura (salmon eggs)

**to serve**
wasabi, pickled ginger and soy sauce

First prepare the mooli salad following the instructions on page 45 and place it in the refrigerator to crisp.

Cut all of the fish into sashimi pieces following the techniques on pages 19, 26 and 33 respectively. You will need twelve slices of each fish. Keep any off-cuts to make tartar or maki rolls.

Drain the mooli salad and divide it among four serving plates. Arrange three pieces of salmon so that they overlap and lay them together on the plate. Repeat with the tuna and mackerel, then spoon one-quarter of the ikura onto each plate. Serve with the wasabi, pickled ginger and soy sauce.

Tip: I also like to serve this dish with mixed baby salad leaves. To do this, divide 100g salad leaves between the serving plates, top with the mooli salad, scatter the fish across and finish with fresh herbs such as shiso, chives or coriander.

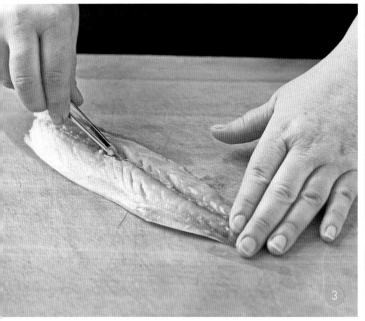

# preparing mackerel and other small round fish

Marinating mackerel and other wild, small round fish helps preserve the flesh, makes it safe to eat and easy to cut. Farmed sea bass does not need marinating: fillet it in the same manner, then remove the skin.

1. Start with a fish that has been gutted and had its head removed. Cut along the back and belly of the fish, into the spine. Then hold the fish flat against the board and, keeping the knife flat, cut horizontally along the side of the spine to loosen the top fillet. Repeat on the other side.

2. Working at a 45-degree angle, trim off the thin white tissue layer, keeping as much flesh on the fillet as possible.

3. Use tweezers to remove the pin bones left in the fillet.

4. Place the fillets skin-side down in a baking tray or similar and sprinkle coarse sea salt over them. Set the fish aside for 30 minutes, then rinse off the salt and pat the fillets dry with kitchen paper.

5. Put 300ml sushi vinegar, 20ml soy sauce and a piece of kombu in a large dish. Lay the fillets skin-side up in the mixture and leave to marinate for 20 minutes. Position a cutting board at an angle by sitting an upturned plate under one side. Lay the marinated fillets on the board to drain for a few minutes.

6. Reposition the board so that it is flat. Starting at the bottom corner of each fillet, carefully peel off the papery white outer skin, leaving the silver patterned skin on the fillet. Slice the fish into sashimi and nigiri pieces by working diagonally along the fillet while at the same time cutting downwards at a 45-degree angle.

# sea bass sashimi with chilli oil

serves • • • •

For this dish I favour young sea bass as they have firmer flesh than the older fish. Use a good sustainably-farmed sea bass or, if you are using a wild fish, freeze the sea bass fillets for a few hours to eliminate any contamination from fish worm or parasites. Sea bass is a fish that keeps well even when bought filleted, so you could ask the fishmonger to do the hard work. The chilli oil needs to be made at least one day in advance of serving and will last for up to two months stored in a cool cupboard or fridge.

400g Mooli Salad (see page 45)
small bunch of coriander
100g mixed baby salad leaves
2 small-medium sea bass

**for the chilli oil**
6 large red chillies
200ml olive oil

**to serve**
wasabi, pickled ginger and soy sauce

To make the chilli oil: cut the chillies straight down the middle, scrape out and discard the seeds and cut the flesh into chunky pieces. Put the chilli in a shallow ovenproof tray, cover with the olive oil and cook at 70°C/Gas $1/2$ for 1 hour. Leave to rest for a day, then strain the mixture and decant the oil into a squeeze bottle.

Prepare the mooli salad following the recipe on page 45 and place in the fridge to crisp. Meanwhile, pick 20 perfect leaves from the bunch of coriander and set them aside on a piece of kitchen paper.

Divide the baby salad leaves among four serving plates and top with the drained mooli salad.

Fillet the sea bass using the technique on page 32 and skin the fillets. Cut each fillet on the bias to give 5-6 slices per fillet. Place a whole fillet of sea bass on each plate, arranging the slices so that they overlap one another.

Insert a single coriander leaf between each slice of fish, then drizzle with the chilli oil and serve with wasabi, pickled ginger and soy sauce.

Tip: very good quality ready-made chilli oils are widely available. I like the Japanese brand La-Yu, made by S&B.

# mr shibushi's mackerel sashimi

serves ● ● ● ●

This is my tribute to my fish mentor Mr Shibushi, who always takes good care of me when I am in Tokyo. We go together to the fish market in the morning, talk to the best tuna traders and eat the freshest tuna sashimi I have ever had, served with strong black coffee in one of the small sushi stalls surrounding the market. I will pick a fish I find interesting, then we will return to The Quarter House in Akasaka and Mr Shibushi will talk me through every step of preparing this fish. I speak very little Japanese, but food is an international language. 'Watch and learn' has taught me some of my fundamental fish carving skills. Since I met Mr Shibushi in London in 1994 and he taught me to hand-carve mooli, he has opened the world of Japanese cuisine for me, and made me realise that this is a life journey, with ever-new areas and techniques to explore. My gratitude is immense.

4 marinated mackerel (see pages 32-33)
400g Mooli Salad (see page 45)
100g mixed baby salad leaves
12 long chives
1 punnet shiso cress
50g mixed black and white sesame
    seeds

**to serve**
wasabi, pickled ginger and soy sauce

Marinate the mackerel using the techniques on pages 32-33. Meanwhile, prepare the mooli salad following the recipe on page 45 and place in the fridge to crisp.

Pull the clear membrane from each fillet of mackerel and cut on the bias to give 7-8 slices per fillet.

Divide the baby salad leaves among four serving plates and place the mooli salad on top. Arrange the mackerel on top of the mooli so that the slices of fish overlap one another.

Decorate each plate of sashimi with three spears of chives, a cluster of shiso cress and finally a sprinkling of black and white sesame seeds. Serve the mackerel with the wasabi, pickled ginger and soy sauce.

# scallop sashimi to dive for

serves ● ● ● ●

Scallops are particularly good during the winter months because the colder sea makes them both fresher and safer. It is worth the wait for these tight, succulent pieces of flesh. It pains me to walk along a harbour front seeing the big rusty iron cast nets used for scallop fishing as they literally scrape the sea bed of its life and leave only destruction behind. Fishing for scallops like this is unnecessary and the end product is either frozen or kept in brine, turning them into big fluffy balls. I will only use hand-dived scallops, which makes them a little tricky to get hold of if the weather is very cold and the sea is rough – conditions that are bad for diving. This simple recipe highlights the succulent texture of truly fresh scallops. Buy them ready-shelled from the best fishmonger in your area.

400g Mooli Salad (see page 45)
small handful of coriander
8 scallops
40ml olive oil
4 teaspoons sesame oil
80g mixed black and white sesame seeds
2 spring onions, finely sliced at an angle

**to serve**
wasabi, pickled ginger and soy sauce

Prepare the mooli salad following the recipe on page 45 and place in the fridge to crisp. Pick the leaves from the coriander and set them aside on a piece of kitchen paper.

Clean the scallops as necessary, removing the intestines and corals. Rinse and pat dry with kitchen paper. Slice each scallop horizontally into three discs.

Drain the mooli salad and divide it among four serving plates. Arrange six pieces of scallop so that they overlap one another and sit them on top of the mooli salad.

In a small saucepan, heat the olive and sesame oils together until smoking point is reached. Drizzle the oil over the sashimi. Sprinkle with the black and white sesame seeds, spring onions and coriander leaves, then serve with wasabi, pickled ginger and soy sauce.

# prawn ceviche

As with all shellfish, freshness is the key word here. This recipe is not strictly a ceviche, but the name does emphasise the importance of using only the freshest and best quality prawns. The term 'size 16/20' means that there will be 16 to 20 prawns per kilogram.

200g Mooli Salad (see page 45)
20 raw tiger prawns, size 16/20
1/2 cucumber
2 stalks celery, destrung
1 small red onion, finely sliced
1 pink grapefruit

**for the ceviche marinade**
2 passionfruit
4 teaspoons ponzu sauce
1 tablespoon red wine vinegar
1 tablespoon honey

If you have not already done so, make a half quantity of the mooli salad on page 45 and place in the fridge to crisp.

Peel the prawns and remove the intestinal threads. Run a skewer through each one to stretch out the body (see picture page 71). Cook the skewered prawns for 4 minutes in a pan of boiling salted water, then plunge immediately into cold water to help preserve the colour and flavour.

For the ceviche marinade: halve the passionfruit and scrape the seeds and juice into a bowl. Add the ponzu sauce, vinegar and honey and stir well.

When the prawns have cooled, remove the skewers and cut each prawn diagonally into four pieces. Add them to the ceviche marinade and set aside for 10 minutes.

Halve and deseed the cucumber. Cut it diagonally into thin slices and place in a mixing bowl. Cut the celery into very thin julienne about 4cm long and add to the mixing bowl with the finely sliced onion. Peel and segment the grapefruit and add the segments to the bowl.

Add half the prawn mixture to the salad and mix gently. Divide among four serving plates, then top with the remaining prawns. Use the excess marinade as a salad dressing and drizzle it over the dish before serving.

# salads

Traditional Japanese salads tend to be small and tasty, comprising just a few ingredients such as seaweed, pickles, mooli, spinach and sesame seeds, plus a good dressing. However in Japan it is increasingly fashionable to use vegetables like cherry tomatoes and bell peppers for crunch and flavour. My principle when developing salads for Feng Sushi is that they must include at least three true Japanese ingredients, but the simple, healthy recipes that follow also have a European accent.

Ikura potato salad

## dashi dressing

makes 150ml

1 tablespoon dashi powder
1 tablespoon honey
2 teaspoons soy sauce
2 teaspoons sushi vinegar
1 teaspoon wasabi paste
2 tablespoons olive oil
2 tablespoons sunflower oil
4 teaspoons sesame oil

Combine the dashi, honey,
soy sauce, sushi vinegar
and wasabi in a small food
processor bowl or beaker and
blend briefly. Mix the olive,
sunflower and sesame oils
together and gradually add
them to the dashi mixture,
blending until smooth. This
dressing will keep for a week
in the fridge.

## japanese thousand island dressing

makes 250ml

200ml Feng Mayo
  (see page 44)
4 teaspoons spring water
4 teaspoons yuzu juice
2 teaspoons kimchee base

Make a batch of Feng Mayo as
described in the recipe overleaf.
Then add the spring water, yuzu
juice and kimchee base to the
food processor and continue
blending for 1 minute or until
the mixture is smooth. This
dressing will keep for up to
five days in the fridge.

## japanese vinaigrette

makes 200ml

2 tablespoons yuzu juice
2 tablespoons sushi vinegar
1 tablespoon wasabi paste
2 teaspoons sweet chilli sauce,
  or 1 teaspoon honey
100ml sunflower, grapeseed or
  vegetable oil
50ml extra virgin olive oil

Combine the yuzu juice, vinegar,
wasabi and sweet chilli sauce
or honey in a small food
processor bowl or beaker and
blend until the mixture is
smooth and light green.

Mix the two oils together in
a measuring jug, then add
gradually to the wasabi mixture
while the machine is running,
blending until the dressing has
a consistency similar to French
vinaigrette. This dressing will
keep for up to two weeks in the
refrigerator.

## miso dressing

makes 200ml

1 shallot, finely chopped
1 large clove garlic, finely chopped
3 tablespoons white miso paste
juice of 1 lemon
1 tablespoon wholegrain mustard
2 teaspoons pumpkinseed oil, or
  sesame oil
1 teaspoon balsamic vinegar
1/2 tablespoon honey
70ml sunflower oil
2 tablespoons extra virgin olive oil

Put the shallot and garlic in a
small food processor with the
miso, lemon juice, mustard,
pumpkinseed (or sesame) oil,
balsamic vinegar and honey
and blend briefly to combine.

Mix the sunflower and olive oils
together in a jug then turn the
machine on and gradually add
the oils to the miso mixture,
blending until the dressing has
the consistency of a thick
vinaigrette – you may not need
all the oil. This dressing will
keep for a week in the fridge.

## tahini dressing

makes 200 ml

180ml crème fraîche
juice of 1/2 lemon
1 tablespoon tahini
1 tablespoon runny honey
1 teaspoon cumin
pinch of cayenne pepper
freshly ground salt and pepper

Combine all the ingredients in
a mixing bowl and stir until
well blended. This dressing will
keep for three days in the fridge.

## scandia dill dressing

makes 200ml

100g fresh dill sprigs
180ml crème fraîche
juice of 1/2 lemon
1 teaspoon wasabi paste
1/2 teaspoon caster sugar
freshly ground salt and pepper

Discard the stalks of the dill,
then rinse the remainder
thoroughly in cold water and
pat dry with a tea towel. Chop
the dill fronds finely and place
in a mixing bowl. Add the
crème fraiche, lemon juice,
wasabi, caster sugar and salt
and pepper and mix well. This
dressing will keep for three
days in the fridge.

## simple teriyaki

makes 250ml

125ml soy sauce
70ml mirin
70ml sake
100g caster sugar
2-3 teaspoons cornflour

Gently heat the soy sauce, mirin, sake and sugar together in a small saucepan, being sure not to let it boil as this will make the soy sauce black and granulated. Meanwhile, in a small dish, blend the cornflour with 20ml cold water.

When the sugar has dissolved in the soy liquid, add a third of the slaked cornflour, whisking constantly as you do so. Repeat this process until the soy mixture is silky smooth and has a consistency similar to double cream. Leave the dressing to cool, then store in fridge, where it will keep for up to two weeks.

Tip: teriyaki sauce will thicken after a couple of days in the fridge, so place it in a saucepan over a low heat, add a splash of soy sauce and a splash of mirin, and give it a good whisk to return the sauce to a silky smooth consistency.

## feng mayo

makes 200ml

1 whole free range egg
2 free range egg yolks
2 tablespoons caster sugar
2 teaspoons sushi vinegar
100ml sunflower, grapeseed or vegetable oil
50ml extra virgin olive oil

Combine the whole egg, yolks, caster sugar and sushi vinegar in a small food processor bowl or beaker and blend until white and fluffy. Mix the two oils together in a jug and add to the egg mixture gradually, while the machine is running, to give a rich even mayonnaise. This dressing will keep for up to three days in the fridge.

Tip: I advise using free range eggs from salmonella-free flocks, however it is generally recommended that people who are pregnant or in a vulnerable health group avoid dishes containing raw eggs.

## feng pesto

makes 200ml

50g pine nuts
100g coriander sprigs
80g basil sprigs
1 large clove garlic
2 teaspoons sweet chilli sauce, or 1 teaspoon honey
2 tablespoons sunflower, grapeseed or vegetable oil
4 teaspoons extra virgin olive oil

Toast the pine nuts in a dry frying pan over medium heat, stirring often, until golden. Transfer the pine nuts to kitchen paper to cool down. Place the herbs in a food processor with the toasted pine nuts, garlic and sweet chilli sauce (or honey).

Combine the two oils in a small dish. Turn the machine on and gradually add the oils, blending until the pesto is well mixed – you may not need all the oil. This pesto will keep for up to three days in the fridge.

Tip: the herbs can be replaced with fresh parsley, chervil, chives or young rocket leaves. I do not add parmesan to this pesto as the cheese would overpower the raw fish.

# mooli salad

serves ● ● ● ●

Mooli, sometimes called daikon or Chinese radish, is a large white radish traditionally used to accompany sashimi. It is an important part of the balance of a Japanese meal as it helps digestion and fat burning, is rich in vitamin C, and can even prevent heartburn. It is also very tasty. I like to add cucumber to the standard mooli salad for extra colour and crispness, and grate both vegetables using a Japanese turner, which makes long curly strands that look good piled high on the plate. This recipe makes about 400g of salad.

1 large mooli
1 cucumber

Peel the mooli and cut into four blocks. Place one block at a time on a Japanese turner, or a mandolin, and grate the mooli into a bowl.

Cut the cucumber into thirds and grate each piece on the turner or mandolin as you did with the mooli, discarding the seeds as you go.

Carefully mix the vegetables together, then cover with tap water and add a handful of ice cubes. Place in the fridge for at least 30 minutes.

Drain the mooli salad – it should be almost translucent and very crisp. It will last for a day covered in water in the fridge, but if you are making it this far in advance, be sure to give it a couple of rinses under cold running water before draining and serving, as the radish will develop a very sharp smell.

Tip: Japanese turners are available from most catering outlets, I prefer to use the medium blade, so that the vegetables are not too chunky but still have a good crunch.

# japanese bean salad

serves ● ● ● ●

Edamame are young soy beans and an excellent source of protein. Readily available frozen in Asian stores and supermarkets, they are traditionally served steamed in their shells with a sprinkling of sea salt, or a mirin dip. However as this dish shows, they also make an excellent salad ingredient. For the mixed salad leaves required in this and the following recipes, choose what you prefer from leaves such as baby chard, red mustard, mizuna, baby spinach and young rocket. Cherry tomatoes are generally best from the middle to end of the summer and have the most flavour when bought on the vine.

100g mixed baby salad leaves
500g frozen edamame
200g frozen broad beans
300g cherry tomatoes on the vine
300g feta cheese
freshly ground pepper

**to serve**
100ml Miso Dressing
   (see page 43)

Prepare the miso dressing using the method on page 43 then decant the dressing into a squeeze bottle. Gently rinse the salad leaves and leave to rest in a colander.

Put a kettle of water on to boil. Place the unshelled edamame in a large heatproof bowl and cover with the hot water from the kettle. Let the edamame steep for 5 minutes, then drain in a colander and pod the beans as soon as they are cool enough to handle.

Meanwhile, bring a saucepan of salted water to the boil and cook the frozen broad beans for 3 minutes. Drain and immediately plunge the broad beans into ice-cold water to help them retain their bright green colour. Rinse the cherry tomatoes and cut each one in half.

In a large bowl, combine the salad leaves, edamame, broad beans and tomatoes. Crumble the feta cheese over the salad. Drizzle with the prepared miso dressing and season with pepper. Arrange the salad on four plates or in a salad bowl and serve as a light lunch.

# ikura potato salad

serves ● ● ● ●

Originating in the Americas, potatoes remain a relatively foreign ingredient in the Japanese kitchen, even though they have become a part of the staple diet in Northern Europe. All through my childhood the first small spuds to grow to an eatable size each year were awaited with much anticipation and excitement – they were a real sign that summer had arrived. This salad works best with fresh baby potatoes such as charlotte or juliette.

1kg baby potatoes
100g mixed baby salad leaves
500g frozen edamame
small bunch of chives
zest of $1/2$ lemon
120g ikura (salmon eggs)

**to serve**
100ml Scandia Dill Dressing (see page 43)

Make the Scandia Dill Dressing according to the recipe on page 43 and set aside. Cook the potatoes in boiling salted water until just tender. Drain, then rinse the potatoes a couple of times in cold water, and leave to dry and cool for at least half an hour.

Meanwhile, prepare the rest of the ingredients. Put a kettle of water on to boil. Rinse the salad leaves gently in cold water and leave to drain in a colander. Place the unshelled edamame in a large heatproof bowl and cover with the hot water from the kettle. Leave for 5 minutes, then drain and pod the edamame. Cut the chives into 5cm pieces.

When the potatoes are ready, cut them in half and place in a large bowl with the salad leaves, edamame, chives, lemon zest. Add the Scandia dill dressing and ikura and toss well. Arrange on four plates or in a salad bowl and serve as a light lunch.

# soba noodle salad

serves ● ● ● ●

Soba noodles make an excellent alternative to pasta in salads. They taste delicious and are particularly healthy because they are made from buckwheat, which is a source of slow-releasing carbohydrate. This salad is super simple, but very nutritious.

100g soba noodles
100g chasoba (green tea soba noodles)
100g pine nuts
80g rocket leaves
1/2 bunch spring onions

**to serve**
100ml Japanese Vinaigrette
(see page 42)

Prepare the Japanese vinaigrette as directed on page 42 and decant into a squeeze bottle.

Cook the two varieties of soba together in a large saucepan of boiling salted water for 6-7 minutes, until the noodles are al dente – tender but still with some bite. Drain the noodles and plunge them into ice-cold water for a few minutes to help preserve their flavour, then place them in a colander under a running tap for a minute or so, which will add extra shine to the noodles.

Toast the pine nuts in a dry frying pan over a medium heat, stirring often, until they are golden. Transfer them to a piece of kitchen paper to cool.

Remove any thick stalks from the rocket leaves, rinse gently and set aside to drain in a colander. Trim the spring onions and slice them finely on the diagonal.

In a large salad bowl, combine the noodles, vinaigrette, pine nuts, rocket and spring onions and toss well before serving as a light lunch.

# x-ray salad

serves ● ● ● ●

In 1999, when we opened the first of our restaurants, we sensed that the Low/No Carb movement was about to take hold. In response, we made this delicious salad with crisp translucent mooli, lots of glorious vegetables and named it after the ultra-thin socialites in Tom Wolfe's **Bonfire of the Vanities**. When preparing the mooli salad, use a Japanese turner or mandolin for the best result.

400g Mooli Salad (see page 45)

500g frozen edamame

2 ripe green-skinned avocados

2 large sweet peppers, ideally one red and one yellow

seeds of 1 pomegranate

40g pickled ginger, finely chopped

finely julienned zest of $1/2$ lemon

100g mixed black and white toasted sesame seeds

**to serve**

200ml Japanese Vinaigrette (see page 42)

Prepare the Japanese vinaigrette according to the recipe on page 42 and decant into a squeeze bottle ready to serve.

Make the mooli salad as described on page 45 and place in the fridge to chilli. Meanwhile, bring a kettle of water to the boil. Place the edamame in a heatproof bowl and cover with the hot water from the kettle. Leave to stand for 5 minutes, then drain and pod the beans.

Drain the mooli salad and divide it among four serving plates. Halve, stone and peel the avocados, then cut the flesh into cubes and arrange freely on the top of the mooli salad. Cut the peppers into thin julienne at an angle and discard any seeds or white flesh. Again, arrange these freely on top of the mooli salad.

Sprinkle over the pomegranate seeds, edamame, chopped ginger, lemon zest and sesame seeds. Drizzle with the Japanese vinaigrette and serve.

# miso and poppy seed salmon with rustic sweet potatoes

serves ● ● ● ●

This is my take on miso-marinated fish. For it I use a good quality farmed salmon or even wild salmon, and it is fine to keep the brown flesh of the salmon in this instance as it is both marinated and cooked. Sweet potatoes are good alternative to normal potatoes as they contain less starch, but also add a natural sweetness to the dish. You will need to start this recipe a couple of days in advance of serving.

200g white miso paste

2 tablespoons caster sugar

2 tablespoons mirin

2 tablespoons sake

400g salmon fillets

2 large sweet potatoes

2 lemons

100ml olive oil

2 tablespoons poppy seeds

salt and pepper

100g baby spinach leaves

extra virgin olive oil, for drizzling

Place the miso paste, caster sugar, mirin and sake in a saucepan over a medium heat and stir constantly until the ingredients have all melted. Set aside to cool.

Cut the salmon into 2cm cubes and place in a non-reactive dish. Pour the cooled miso mixture over the fish and marinate in the fridge for 2-3 days.

On the day of serving, preheat the oven to 250°C/Gas 9. Cut the sweet potatoes into 2cm cubes and place on a baking tray. Squeeze the juice from the lemons and combine with the olive oil, poppy seeds and some salt and pepper. Pour this dressing over the sweet potatoes then, for extra flavour, add the lemon skins to the baking tray. Roast for 25-30 minutes or until cooked through.

Take the salmon from the fridge and rinse off the marinade. Line a baking tray with greaseproof paper and place the fish on it. When the sweet potatoes have been cooking for 20 minutes, place the tray of fish in the oven, turn it down to 220°C/Gas 7 and continue cooking.

Divide the baby spinach among serving bowls. When the potatoes and salmon are cooked, remove from the oven and discard the lemon skins. Gently mix the fish and sweet potatoes together and place on top of the spinach. Drizzle with a little extra virgin olive oil and serve as a main course.

# crab claw meat udon noodle salad

serves ● ● ● ●

A dried flat noodle works best in this light lunch or starter dish. Dried udon is a Japanese cousin of Italian taglierini and comes in thin ribbons. Whole crab can be used for this recipe, but I prefer using a good quality pasteurised, ready-picked crab meat such as that sold by Harvey's of Newlyn in Penzance. This makes the salad far less laborious to prepare, but equally tasty.

120g dried udon noodles
1 large, ripe, green-skinned avocado
$1/2$ cucumber
4 spring onions
200g crab claw meat

**to serve**
100ml Japanese Thousand Island
   Dressing (see page 42)

Prepare the Japanese Thousand Island dressing according to the recipe on page 42 and decant into a squeeze bottle.

Cook the udon for 7-8 minutes in a pot of boiling salted water until they are al dente, or tender but with some bite. Rinse the noodles in cold water and set aside in a colander.

Halve and peel the avocado and cut the flesh into 1cm cubes. Cut the cucumber in half lengthways, scrape out the seeds with a teaspoon and slice the flesh thinly. Trim the spring onions and slice them thinly at an angle.

Pick through the crabmeat carefully, checking for any sinewy pieces or bones. Place in a large bowl with the noodles, half the salad dressing and all the other ingredients. Toss well, then serve the salad in individual bowls, drizzling the remaining dressing on top.

# seaweed salad with mooli, edamame and dashi dressing

serves ● ● ● ●

This is pure power food – every ingredient in this salad has beneficial health properties. Seaweed's natural iodine is good for the metabolism and cleansing the blood. Mooli aids digestion and edamame is a low fat protein rich in fibre. Seaweed, dashi and soy sauce are all categorised under the recently discovered 'fifth taste' umami; best described as natural flavour enhancers. Buy your seaweed from Asian or health food stores, where products such as a wakame and kaiso mixture are readily available in dried form.

400g Mooli Salad (see page 45)
50g mixed dried seaweed
400g frozen edamame

**to serve**
120ml Dashi Dressing (see page 42)

Prepare the dashi dressing following the recipe on page 42 and decant it into a squeeze bottle. Then prepare the mooli salad as per the instructions on page 45 and set aside in the bowl of iced water to crisp.

Place the dried seaweed in a bowl, cover with cold water from the tap and leave to soak for 10 minutes. Meanwhile, put a kettle of water on to boil. Place the edamame in a large heatproof bowl and cover with hot water from the kettle. Leave to stand for 5 minutes.

Rinse the seaweed in a colander and set aside to drain. Drain the edamame and remove the beans from the pods as soon as they are cool enough to handle.

Drain the mooli salad and arrange on four serving plates. Divide the seaweed and edamame among the plates, then drizzle with the dashi dressing and serve immediately.

# cornish mackerel ceviche with middle eastern inspired salad and creamy tahini dressing

serves ● ● ● ●

I was looking for a way to combine my two favourite foods, chickpeas and fresh mackerel, and came up with this very tasty salad. You could use dried chickpeas instead of canned. Soak 300g in cold water overnight, then simmer in unsalted water for 40 minutes. Drain and rinse in cold water before proceeding with the recipe below. It's important not to add salt to the cooking water as this will prevent the chickpeas becoming tender.

Prepare the tahini dressing according to the instructions on page 43, then prepare the mackerel as per the instructions on page 33.

Cut the cucumber into three blocks, then lengthways through the middle. Discard the seeds and cut the flesh into julienne, or thin batons. Trim the spring onions, cut each one into three even pieces, then slice into julienne.

Peel the thin membrane from the mackerel fillets. Take four of the fillets and cut into thin strips, slicing across the fillet. Cut the remainder on the bias to give sashimi-style pieces, slicing diagonally at an angle of 45 degrees.

In a salad bowl, mix the baby leaves, drained chickpeas, cucumber, spring onions, and thinly sliced mackerel with two-thirds of the tahini dressing.

Arrange the salad on four serving plates, then put two or three pieces of mackerel sashimi on top. Finish with a dollop of dressing and serve as a light lunch or starter.

5 medium-sized mainated mackerel (see page 33)
1 cucumber
4 spring onions
100g mixed baby leaves
400g can chickpeas, drained

**to serve**
120ml Tahini Dressing (see page 43)

# sushi nigiri

Nigiri (small, oval-shaped portions of rice with a topping) are often regarded as the king of the sushi. The word means 'pressed in the hand', referring to the way in which the nigiri are shaped. In Japan the classic toppings include tuna, mackerel, tiger prawns and tamago omelette, among others, but in the sushi bars of the West salmon nigiri is often the most popular variety. There is also a version called gunkan (meaning 'boat'), that consists of rice balls wrapped with nori and filled with roe such as salmon eggs, or sea urchin. Once you have acquired the basic technique, the possibilities are endless. For extra flavour I like to cure the fish, make tamago with a tasty filling, or add toppings such as chilli oil, pesto, fresh herbs and home-made mayonnaise. For a lunch or light dinner for three to four people, twenty pieces of sushi nigiri will be enough. Start with two or three varieties and, when you have got the knack of it, experiment with different flavours. The recipes in this chapter can easily be cut in half.

Sea bass nigiri with chilli oil and coriander

# shaping nigiri

Traditional sushi chefs shape nigiri entirely by hand, but novices can achieve good, consistent results using a mould. The freshly cooked rice should have cooled to about 28°C before you start. Fill a bowl with water and add a splash of vinegar to it – this is used to prevent the rice sticking to your hands or the mould.

1   Dip your hands and the mould in the acidulated water. Take a small handful of rice and gently press it into the nigiri mould, working it lightly into the corners. Do not press hard or the sushi will be too heavy. I think it is best to fill the mould only about four-fifths so the nigiri are not too big.

2   Attach the back of the mould, turn the mould over and use your thumb to scrape any loose rice away from the holes.

3   Take the back off the mould and turn the rice blocks out on to a board, tapping gently through the holes to free the rice.

4   With the topping in one hand, apply a thin layer of wasabi to the underside of the topping. Pick up a rice block using your other hand and gently remould it by cupping your fingers and thumb around it and pressing three or four times. This helps to prevent the rice falling apart.

5   Bring the rice block and topping together and shape the topping down the sides of the rice using your index finger and thumb. The nigiri should be long yet curvaceous.

6   To make gunkan nigiri, cut pieces of nori into strips measuring 7x2.5cm. Wrap one strip around each block of rice (you don't have to reshape the rice in your hand) and secure it by pressing a couple of grains of rice between the seaweed at the top and bottom of the strip. Then fill the boat you have created with the chosen filling.

# salmon nigiri with ikura

makes

Salmon nigiri is by far the most popular type of nigiri in the West. To enhance the flavour I have added ikura (salmon eggs) for a hint of salt, and cress for a peppery taste. The real fun is the wonderful sensation the ikura gives when the eggs pop in the mouth, making this nigiri perfect to enjoy with a glass of chilled champagne.

400g Prepared Sushi Rice (see page 15)
300g salmon nigiri block (see page 18)
1/2 teaspoon wasabi paste
2 spring onions, thickly sliced at an angle
100g ikura (salmon eggs)
sprigs of mustard cress

**to serve**
wasabi, pickled ginger,
grated mooli and soy sauce

Prepare the sushi rice as described on page 15 and allow it to cool. Meanwhile, cut the block of salmon into 20 pieces about 3cm wide, 7cm long and 2mm thick. Store the fish in the fridge until the rice is ready.

When the sushi rice has cooled down to about 28°C, mould it into 20 rice blocks (see pages 60-61). If you do not have a nigiri mould, the hand-shaped rice blocks should measure about 5cm long, 2cm wide and 2cm tall.

Apply a thin layer of wasabi to each slice of fish, then lay one on each block of rice, wasabi-side down, following the shaping technique in the photographs on page 61.

Scatter some spring onion on of each nigiri, then top with a spoonful of ikura. Garnish with cress and serve with pickled ginger, grated mooli, more wasabi and soy sauce.

## tuna with shichimi and kimchee
Replace the salmon with tuna sliced nigiri-style (see pages 26-27) then top with a drizzle of kimchee base, strips of red pepper, shiso leaves and sprinkle with shichimi powder.

## mackerel with sesame and poppy seeds
Replace the salmon with marinated mackerel (see pages 32-33) then top with shiso and mustard cress and sprinkle with mixed toasted sesame seeds and some poppy seeds.

tuna nigiri with shichimi and kimchee

mackerel nigiri with sesame and poppy seeds

# thai-style gravadlax nigiri

makes

This is a Scandinavian salmon sushi with an Asian twist. Gravadlax is cured salmon, an old way of preserving fish for the winter months and a well known deli food throughout the world. Traditionally the curing could last for months, but this recipe takes just seven days and the end result freezes well should you be left with some fish. I use Japanese sake instead of Scandinavian aquavit (water of life), but vodka is also suitable. You can make a faster version using good quality bought gravadlax or smoked salmon instead.

400g Prepared Sushi Rice (see page 15)
50g Chilli Jam (see page 150), or Feng Pesto (see page 44)

**for the gravadlax**
1 salmon fillet, about 15cm long, scaled
200ml cold sake
2 stalks lemon grass, thinly sliced at an angle
2 garlic cloves, thinly sliced
small piece of ginger, finely chopped
4 kafir lime leaves, torn into small pieces
200g caster sugar
100g fine sea salt
20g basil sprigs
$1/2$ teaspoon wasabi paste

**to serve**
wasabi, pickled ginger and soy sauce

To make the gravadlax: use a sharp knife to pierce the salmon flesh in eight places. Pour the sake into a shallow dish and soak the salmon skin-side up for 20 minutes. Combine the lemon grass, garlic, ginger, and kafir lime leaves in a small bowl, and the sugar and salt in another.

Place the salmon skin-side down on a large sheet of greaseproof paper. Rub the herb mixture into the flesh, then cover with a layer of basil leaves. Pour the sugar and salt mixture over the top. Wrap the salmon tightly in the greaseproof paper, then wrap tightly in three or four layers of cling film. Place in a tray skin-side up and leave to cure in the fridge for seven days.

To finish the nigiri: prepare the rice following the method on page 15. Meanwhile, unwrap the fish and discard the herbs and marinade. Cut the fillet into a 7.5cm block and trim away the skin (you can freeze it for use in other sushi). Slice the gravadlax into nigiri pieces (see pages 18-19).

When the sushi rice has cooled down to about 28°C, mould it into 20 rice blocks (see pages 60-61). If you do not have a nigiri mould, the hand-shaped rice blocks should measure about 5cm long, 2cm wide and 2cm tall.

Apply a thin layer of wasabi to each slice of fish and lay the fish wasabi-side down on the rice, shaping it into nigiri. Add a tiny dot of chilli jam (or pesto) to each nigiri. Serve with the pickled ginger, soy sauce and some more wasabi.

# seared tuna in pepper and sesame crust nigiri

makes

As with the sashimi version of this recipe, the spiced crust adds extra flavour and depth to the clean taste of the fish.

400g Prepared Sushi Rice (see page 15)
100g mixed black and white sesame seeds
300g tuna nigiri block (see page 27)
2 tablespoons cracked black pepper
1 teaspoon sea salt
olive oil, for frying
$1/2$ teaspoon wasabi paste

**to serve**
wasabi, ginger and soy sauce

Cook the sushi rice according to the instructions on page 15. Meanwhile, using a mortar and pestle, crush together the sesame seeds, black pepper and salt, then spread the mixture in a shallow tray.

Cut the tuna block into two equal pieces measuring approximately 12-14cm long, 7cm wide and 3cm deep. Press the sesame mixture onto the long sides of each block, then put aside to set.

When the sushi rice has cooled down to about 28°C, mould it into 20 rice blocks (see pages 60-61). If you do not have a nigiri mould, the hand-shaped rice blocks should measure about 5cm long, 2cm wide and 2cm tall.

Heat a little olive oil in a frying pan and, when smoking hot, fry the two blocks of tuna on each of the four long sides for 1 minute each, so the flesh is seared all around. Leave to rest for a few minutes, then slice the tuna into nigiri pieces.

Apply a thin layer of wasabi to each slice of fish and mould into nigiri as described on pages 60-61, placing the fish wasabi-side down on the rice. Serve with the pickled ginger, soy sauce and some more wasabi

# sea bass with chilli oil and coriander

makes

Buy a good quality farmed sea bass for this sushi and ask your fishmonger to scale and fillet the fish for you. If you want to make your own chilli oil you will need to begin it at least one day in advance of serving, but you could use a good bought chilli oil instead.

50ml Chilli Oil (see page 34)
400g Prepared Sushi Rice (see page 15)
4 small sea bass fillets
$1/2$ teaspoon wasabi paste
20 coriander leaves

**to serve**
wasabi, pickled ginger and soy sauce

If you have not already done so, make the chilli oil according to the recipe on page 34 and decant it into a squeeze bottle.

On the day of serving, cook the sushi rice using the method on page 15. Meanwhile, skin the fish and cut into nigiri slices: you should get five or six slices from each fillet.

When the sushi rice has cooled down to about 28°C, mould it into 20 rice blocks (see pages 60-61). If you do not have a nigiri mould, the hand-shaped rice blocks should measure about 5cm long, 2cm wide and 2cm tall.

Apply a thin layer of wasabi to each slice of fish and place it wasabi-side down on the rice. Mould it into shape as demonstrated on pages 60-61.

Add a coriander leaf to each nigiri and drizzle with chilli oil. Serve with more wasabi, plus pickled ginger and soy sauce.

# tiger prawns with feng mayo, shichimi and kimchee

makes

400g Prepared Sushi Rice (see page 15)
40ml Feng Mayo (see page 44)
2 tablespoons kimchee base
1-1.2kg raw tiger prawns, size 16/20
$^1/_2$ teaspoon wasabi paste
a little shichimi powder, for sprinkling

**to serve**
wasabi, pickled ginger and soy sauce

Cook the sushi rice using the method on page 15. Meanwhile, make the mayo following the recipe on page 44 and decant the sauce into a squeeze bottle. Put the kimchee base into a squeeze bottle too.

To prepare the tiger prawns: tear off the heads, then peel off the shells, leaving the last 'jacket' and tail on each prawn. Carefully pull out the intestinal threads. Skewer the prawns along their bellies, stretching them right to the end of their tails to straighten (see picture below).

Cook the skewered prawns in boiling salted water for 4-5 minutes, until bright pink, then plunge them straight into ice-cold water. When cool, remove the skewers and 'butterfly' the prawns by cutting along the belly side, being careful not to cut the whole way through.

When the sushi rice has cooled down to about 28°C, mould it into 20 rice blocks (see pages 60-61). If you do not have a nigiri mould, the hand-shaped rice blocks should measure about 5cm long, 2cm wide and 2cm tall.

Apply a thin layer of wasabi to the underside of each prawn and mould one prawn over each block of rice. Garnish the nigiri with a dot of Feng Mayo, a dot of kimchee base, and a sprinkling of shichimi powder. Serve with additional wasabi, plus pickled ginger and soy sauce.

# smoked chicken with white asparagus nigiri

makes

Hot smoked chicken is delicious and surprising in this ambitious, meaty nigiri. Smoking at home is easy as long as the process is followed step by step. In Europe, white asparagus is in season from April to late September. For this dish you could also use green asparagus.

100ml Simple Teriyaki Sauce
  (see page 44)
400g Prepared Sushi Rice (see page 15)
2 organic chicken breasts,
  about 220g each
85g demerara sugar
85g raw long grain rice
4 tablespoons green tea
a little olive oil, for drizzling
salt and pepper
1/2 lemon
1 stalk lemon grass
5 spears white asparagus
a few strips of nori
1/2 teaspoon wasabi paste

**to serve**
wasabi and pickled ginger

Make the teriyaki sauce using the recipe on page 44. Meanwhile, cook the sushi rice as described on page 15.

To smoke the chicken: line a wok with a sheet of foil and put a mixture of the sugar, rice and tea in the base. Cover with another sheet of foil and place the wok over a medium heat. When the pan starts to smoke, put the chicken on the foil. Sprinkle with olive oil, salt and pepper, and add the lemon and lemon grass to the wok. Cover with a tight-fitting lid and leave to smoke for about 25 minutes, or until the chicken is tender. Set the cooked chicken aside to rest.

Blanch the asparagus in a tall saucepan of boiling water for 4 minutes, then plunge into ice-cold water to stop the cooking. Cut the asparagus lengthways down the middle, and in half crossways at an angle. Make 20 nori belts by cutting the nori into strips measuring 6cm by 1cm.

When the sushi rice has cooled down to about 28°C, mould it into 20 rice blocks (see pages 60-61). If you do not have a nigiri mould, the hand-shaped rice blocks should measure about 5cm long, 2cm wide and 2cm tall.

Slice the smoked chicken on the bias to give thin slices of similar size to traditional nigiri toppings. Apply a thin layer of wasabi to each slice of chicken and lay wasabi-side down on the rice, shaping them into nigiri (see pages 60-61). Balance a piece of white asparagus on top of each nigiri and secure with a nori belt. Serve with extra wasabi, pickled ginger and the teriyaki sauce.

Prepare the sushi rice following the method on page 15 and allow it to cool.

Meanwhile, cut the beef to a piece about 7cm wide and 2-3cm tall. Trim each end off the block so you have a blunt square to work with. Season the beef on each side. Heat the oil and butter in a non-stick pan. Sear the beef on all four long sides for 2 minutes per side, so the heat penetrates to a depth of 5-7mm on each side. Set aside to rest.

To make the horseradish and wasabi cream: in a small bowl mix the wasabi paste with the Philadelphia cream cheese and horseradish, then set aside.

When the sushi rice has cooled down to about 28°C, mould it into 16 rice blocks (see pages 60-61). If you do not have a nigiri mould, the hand-shaped rice blocks should measure about 5cm long, 2cm wide and 2cm tall.

Thinly slice the beef along the length of the piece (pieces should be about 3cm wide, so it may be necessary to cut at an angle). Apply a thin layer of wasabi to each slice and place on top of the rice blocks, wasabi-side down. Arrange the nigiri on serving plates and top with some spring onion and a dab of the horseradish and wasabi cream.

Dress each plate with a little salad of grated mooli and rocket leaves, topped with another dab of the horseradish and wasabi cream. Serve with extra wasabi, pickled ginger and soy sauce.

400g Prepared Sushi Rice (see page 15)
1 piece beef topside or sirloin, about 300g
sea salt and freshly ground black pepper
1 teaspoon olive oil
small knob of butter
$1/2$ teaspoon wasabi paste
2 spring onions, thickly sliced at an angle

for the fresh horseradish
and wasabi cream
$1/2$ teaspoon wasabi paste
100g Philadelphia Lite cream cheese
2 tablespoons finely grated fresh
  horseradish or good-quality bottled
  horseradish

to serve
grated mooli, rocket leaves, wasabi,
  pickled ginger, soy sauce

# organic beef nigiri with fresh horseradish and wasabi cream

serves • • • •

The Japanese appreciate beef, particularly their famous Kobe beef, with its wonderful marbling. Britain has equally great organic sirloin and, as with Kobe beef, it commands a premium price. The beef in this recipe is all but raw, so needs to be of a very high standard. Ask a reliable butcher to give you a special cut of topside, ideally a block about 3cm tall, 7cm wide and 10cm long. Alternatively, cut a good steak to size. This nigiri makes a show-stopping starter.

# crab gunkan with avocado and wasabi mayo

makes ⦂⦂⦂⦂⦂

For this recipe I use green-skinned avocados as they keep their shape when sliced or diced; black-skinned varieties are better for dishes in which the avocado is mashed, such as guacamole. I do not believe that drizzling pre-cut avocado with lemon juice helps preserve its colour, therefore I only cut avocado 'to order', just before it is being served. When making this nigiri, be sure to choose good quality hand-picked crabmeat from a reliable supplier, to save yourself the hard labour of cleaning the crab.

200g Prepared Sushi Rice (see page 15)
50ml Feng Mayo (see page 44)
1 teaspoon wasabi powder
150g white crabmeat
a few strips of nori
1/2 ripe, green-skinned avocado

**to serve**
wasabi, pickled ginger, and soy sauce

Cook the rice according to the instructions on page 15. Meanwhile, if you have not already done so, make the Feng Mayo using the recipe on page 44. Dilute the wasabi powder in a few drops of cold water, add it to the mayo and place the sauce in a squeeze bottle ready for garnishing.

Carefully pick over the crabmeat to check for any remnants of shell or cartilage. Cut the nori into belts measuring 2.5cm by 8cm. Halve the avocado, then peel it and cut the flesh into tiny squares.

When the sushi rice has cooled down to about 28°C, mould it into ten rice blocks (see pages 60-61). If you do not have a nigiri mould, the hand-shaped rice blocks should measure about 5cm long, 2cm wide and 2cm tall.

Wrap a nori belt around each rice block so that they look like little boats. Seal the nori by pressing it together with a few grains of cooked sushi rice.

Fill the gunkan a quarter full with diced avocado, and the reminder with crabmeat. Decorate with a dot of wasabi mayo and a few pieces of diced avocado. Serve with soy sauce, pickled ginger and wasabi.

Tip: For the nori belts you can use off-cuts from making maki and therefore minimise wastage.

# ikura gunkan

makes • • • • •
• • • • •

This is the most famous gunkan nigiri: simple salmon eggs inside a crisp nori wrapper. Japanese salmon eggs (ikura) are salted or marinated in soy. Any good quality salmon eggs are good for this recipe – as long as you are willing to pay the premium prices.

200g Prepared Sushi Rice (see page 15)
a few strips of nori
150g ikura (salmon eggs)
10 long chives, halved, or 20 short chives

**to serve**
wasabi, pickled ginger and soy sauce

Cook the rice following the method on page 15. Meanwhile, cut the nori into belts measuring 2.5cm by 8cm and cut the chives into 5cm pieces.

When the rice has cooled down to about 28°C, mould it into ten rice blocks (see pages 60-61). Wrap a nori belt around each rice block, sealing the edges with a few rice grains.

Carefully fill each gunkan boat with a heaped teaspoon of salmon eggs, then decorate each one with two short chives. Serve with wasabi, pickled ginger and soy sauce.

# tuna tartar with wasabi tobiko

makes • • • • •
• • • • •

200g Prepared Sushi Rice (see page 15)
4 teaspoons Feng Mayo (see page 44)
200g tuna off-cuts, minced (see page 27)
1 tablespoon ponzu sauce
1 spring onion, very finely chopped
a few strips of nori
40g wasabi tobiko

**to serve**
wasabi, pickled ginger and soy sauce

Cook the rice using the method on page 15. Meanwhile, make the Feng Mayo according to the recipe on page 44.

Mix the minced tuna with the ponzu sauce, 2 teaspoons of the mayo and the spring onions. Cut the nori into belts measuring 2.5cm by 8cm.

When the rice has cooled down to about 28°C, mould it into ten rice blocks (see pages 60-61). Wrap a nori belt around each rice block, sealing the edges with a few rice grains.

Fill each gunkan with a heaped teaspoon of the tuna tartar and decorate with a dot of mayo and the wasabi tobiko. Serve with the wasabi, pickled ginger and soy sauce.

# scallops seared in teriyaki sauce

makes ⬤⬤⬤⬤⬤
⬤⬤⬤⬤⬤

I use only the freshest scallops for this dish – not scallops kept in brine or frozen, as these tend to absorb 50 percent of their weight in water. The best way of telling the difference is that fresh scallops are smaller and have hint of grey, whereas brine-soaked or frozen scallops look bright white, almost as though they have been bleached.

200g Prepared Sushi Rice (see page 15)
50ml Simple Teriyaki Sauce (see page 44)
a few strips of nori
5 fresh hand-dived scallops

**to serve**
wasabi, pickled ginger and soy sauce

Cook the rice using the method on page 15. Meanwhile, make the teriyaki sauce as described on page 44 and decant it into a squeeze bottle ready for garnishing. Cut the nori into belts measuring 2.5cm by 8cm.

Clean the scallops, removing the corals. Rinse the muscle meat under a cold tap and cut in half.

When the sushi rice has cooled down to about 28°C, mould it into ten rice blocks (see pages 60-61). If you do not have a nigiri mould, the hand-shaped rice blocks should measure about 5cm long, 2cm wide and 2cm tall.

Wrap a nori belt around each rice block, sealing the seaweed with a few rice grains.

Fill each gunkan with half a scallop and drizzle with a little of the teriyaki sauce. Serve the nigiri with the wasabi, pickled ginger and soy sauce.

# tamago

I think you will find this method for tamagoyaki (rolled Japanese omelette) much easier than the traditional technique. Nevertheless you still need to be patient – this dish should not be rushed, but performed in a calm, Zen-like state of mind.

Gently whisk together 6 organic eggs, 2 teaspoons sugar, 1 teaspoon mirin, 1 teaspoon sake and $1/2$ teaspoon light soy sauce, being careful not to add too much air to the mixture. Strain it into a jug to remove any threads of egg white.

1. Place a square tamago pan over a medium heat and use a brush to grease it lightly with sunflower oil.

2. Pour a quarter of the egg mixture evenly over the base of the pan and cook until the top has just set.

3. Using a spatula, fold the omelette lengthways four times, trying to keep the roll as neat and tight as possible.

4. Remove the cylinder of omelette from the pan and put it to one side on a plate. Lightly oil the pan and pour another quarter of the egg mixture over the base.

5. When the second layer of omelette has set, place the rolled omelette back in the pan and wrap the second layer of omelette around it to create a larger roll. Use the spatula to make it as neat as possible, then remove the omelette from the pan. Repeat with the remaining egg mixture.

6. Place the omelette in a bamboo mat and leave to cool for at least 30 minutes. Use a very sharp knife to cut the omelette into ten slices. The omelette can be made a day in advance and kept in the fridge overnight, which also makes it easier to cut.

# tamago with red roasted peppers

makes ⋮⋮⋮⋮⋮

Filling Japanese omelette with Italian ingredients makes an astonishing vegetarian dish.

200g Prepared Sushi Rice (see page 15)

1 roasted red pepper, deseeded and finely sliced

1 teaspoon balsamic vinegar

10 long chives

**for the omelette**

6 medium organic eggs

2 teaspoon sugar

1 teaspoon mirin

1 teaspoon sake

$^1/_2$ teaspoon light soy

vegetable oil, for greasing

**to serve**

wasabi, pickled ginger and soy sauce

Cook the sushi rice according to the instructions on page 15. Meanwhile, put the sliced roast pepper a small bowl and dress with the balsamic vinegar.

Prepare the omelette mixture and begin cooking as shown on pages 80-81, pouring one-quarter of the egg mixture into the pan. Place the roast pepper strips in a line down the first sheet of omelette. When set, fold the omelette into a cylinder, making it as tight as possible, and remove it from the pan. Pour another quarter of the egg mixture into the pan and continue cooking as described on the previous page. When done, leave the omelette to cool down in a rolled bamboo mat for at least 30 minutes.

When the sushi rice has cooled to about 28°C, mould it into ten rice blocks (see pages 60-61). If you do not have a nigiri mould, the hand-shaped rice blocks should measure about 5cm long, 2cm wide and 2cm tall. When the omelette is cool, cut it into ten slices.

Place a piece of tamago on top of each rice block and tie a chive around it to secure. Serve the nigiri with wasabi, pickled ginger and soy sauce.

## tamago with ricotta and spinach

Follow the recipe above but replace the roast pepper filling with this mixture: Cook 100g baby spinach leaves in a lightly oiled frying pan for a few minutes until wilted. Drain thoroughly to remove the excess liquid. Crumble 20g ricotta over the spinach and season with salt and pepper. Fill and complete the omelette as described above then leave to cool. After topping the rice blocks with the sliced omelette, tie a belt of nori around the nigiri to secure them.

# avocado with chives and pressed spinach with sesame seeds

makes ▦

Although these sushi are suitable for vegan diets, all the ingredients widely available.

400g Prepared Sushi Rice (see page 15)

a few strips of nori

**for the spinach topping**

2 tablespoons olive oil

1 tablespoon sesame oil

500g baby spinach leaves

2 tablespoons black sesame seeds,
   toasted

sea salt and pepper

**for the avocado topping**

25 long chives

1 large green skinned avocado

**to serve**

wasabi, pickled ginger and soy sauce

Cook the sushi rice according to the method on page 15.
Meanwhile, prepare the spinach topping: heat the oils in a
wok over medium heat and, when smoking hot, add the
spinach to the pan a handful at a time. Cook, stirring, until
thoroughly wilted. Remove from the heat, add the sesame
seeds and season with salt and pepper.

Place a rolling mat on a couple of layers of kitchen paper
and place a piece of greaseproof paper on top. Put the
spinach on the greaseproof paper and use the mat to press
the spinach into a square log.

Hold the spinach log upright over the sink and gently
squeeze out as much liquid as possible. Replace the paper
towel and greaseproof paper with fresh sheets, then leave
the spinach to rest in the rolling mat for 20 minutes.

For the avocado topping: cut the chives into 5cm pieces.
Halve the avocado, discard the stone and peel off the skin.
Slice each half into five pieces.

When the sushi rice has cooled down to about 28°C, mould
it into 20 rice blocks (see pages 60-61). If you do not have a
nigiri mould, the hand-shaped rice blocks should measure
about 5cm long, 2cm wide and 2cm tall.

Cut the strips of nori into 20 belts measuring 6cm by 1cm.
Take ten blocks of rice and place a slice of avocado on top
of each. Add a bundle of trimmed chives and secure each
nigiri with a nori belt.

Carefully cut the pressed spinach into ten slices. Place one
on each of the remaining rice blocks and secure with a
nori belt. Serve with wasabi, pickled ginger and soy sauce.

# sushi-maki

We must thank Japan's gambling dens for sushi-maki. Card sharks who couldn't bear to leave the table took to wrapping their snacks in rice and nori. They could then graze while keeping their gaze fixed on the game, without the cards sticking to their fingers.

**Clockwise from the top:** Seared Salmon and Red Pepper Maki; Tuna, Spring Onion and Shiso Maki; Scallop, Chive and Shiso Maki; Avocado, Pesto and Chilli Maki; Salmon and Rocket Maki; Brown Rice, Avocado and Cucumber Maki

# rolling sushi-maki

1. Trim each sheet of nori down by cutting a 3.5cm strip along the longest side to give a sheet measuring 15.5 x 20.5cm. Save the off-cuts for making gunkan nigiri and nori belts. Lay your first sheet of nori shiny-side down on a rolling mat and position it so that is close to you, near the edge of the work surface.

2. When the cooked sushi rice has reached a temperature of 28°C, gently spread about 125g of it over the nori, leaving a 1cm border along the side furthest from you free of rice. Be careful not to exert too much pressure on the rice as you spread it, as this may spoil the texture. Spread a line of wasabi paste along the rice about one-third of the way across it from you.

3. Arrange the maki filling on top of the strip of wasabi.

4. Using your thumbs to lift the bamboo mat and your index fingers to hold the filling in place, roll the sushi up and over to form a neat cylinder. Seal the roll with the uncovered border of nori.

5. Press the bamboo slats of the rolling mat along the sides of the sushi roll to shape it into a neat, square-sided maki. Set aside to rest for a few minutes.

6. Remove the sushi roll from the rolling mat and (unless the recipe says otherwise) trim off the rough ends. Finally, cut the roll into eight pieces.

# mixed maki   serves ● ● ● ●

Once you have mastered the basic maki-rolling technique using the simple combinations of fillings given here, feel free to try others. Some suggestions: minced raw tuna with shichimi powder and shiso; off-cuts of tamago with chives and baby spinach; roast red peppers with blanched asparagus; cucumber with pesto and sesame seeds. For any of these rolls, you could replace the white rice with brown (see page 96) if preferred.

600g Prepared Sushi Rice (see page 15)

1 teaspoon Simple Teriyaki Sauce (see page 44)

1 teaspoon Feng Pesto (see page 44)

1/4 green-skinned avocado

1/2 cucumber

1/4 red bell pepper

1 spring onion, green tops only

40g sashimi-grade salmon

40g cooked salmon

40g sashimi-grade tuna

2 hand-dived scallops

5 sheets nori

1/2 teaspoon wasabi paste

small handful of rocket leaves

small handful of shiso cress

5 long chives

2-3 pinches shichimi powder

**to serve**
wasabi, pickled ginger and soy sauce

Cook the sushi rice following the instructions on page 15. Meanwhile, if you have not already done so, prepare the teriyaki and pesto sauces using the recipes on page 44 and place each one in a squeeze bottle.

Cut the piece of avocado into three wedges. Quarter the piece of cucumber lengthways and remove the seeds. Cut the red bell pepper and the green tops of the spring onion into long, thin strips.

Trim any brown bits from the raw, sashimi-grade salmon and cut the flesh into strips. Cut the poached salmon and raw tuna into strips too, keeping them well separated.

Remove the intestines and corals from the scallops, then rinse them in cold water and pat dry with kitchen paper. Cut each scallop into three discs.

Trim each sheet of nori down by one-fifth. Place one sheet on a rolling mat shiny side down and spread about 120g of the cooled sushi rice over it, leaving a 1cm border at the top free of rice (see techniques on page 89). Be careful not to press too hard as this may ruin the rice.

Spread a line of wasabi paste across the very middle of the rice. Lay the raw salmon strips and some rocket leaves on top of this line. Hold the filling in place with your index fingers and roll the nori sheet over to make a cylinder, sealing the roll with the tab of uncovered nori. Use the slats of the rolling mat to square up the roll and set aside to rest for a few minutes.

Repeat the process with the remaining ingredients, using the following combinations for subsequent sheets of nori: tuna, spring onion and shiso; scallop, chives and teriyaki sauce; poached salmon and red pepper; avocado, pesto and shichimi powder.

Cut each maki roll into six pieces and serve with the wasabi, pickled ginger and soy sauce.

Tip: for the cooked salmon you could use poached fish or (as I have done in the picture on page 86) use leftovers from making the seared salmon sashimi on page 22.

# salmon skin with spring onions

makes

When you try this crisp filling for the first time it quickly becomes apparent why it is known as the 'bacon of the sea'. Ask your fishmonger to scale your salmon fillet before he skins it – the skin should be thrown in for free but as many people don't want it, you may have to remind him. Salmon skin freezes well too, so bear this in mind when buying salmon for other dishes. For extra flavour you can use the skin left over from marinating gravadlax; do not worry if there is a little meat on the back as this just adds to the flavour.

500g Prepared Sushi Rice (see page 15)
skin of 1 salmon fillet
salt and pepper
splash of olive oil
4 sheets nori
2 spring onions, finely chopped
60g mizuna leaves

**to serve**
wasabi, pickled ginger and soy sauce

Cook the sushi rice following the instructions on page 15. Meanwhile, cut the salmon skin into eight pieces and season with salt and pepper. Heat a generous splash of olive oil in a non-stick frying pan and fry the salmon skin until light golden. Set aside to drain on kitchen paper to remove any excess oil.

Trim each sheet of nori down by one-fifth. Place one sheet on a rolling mat shiny side down and spread about 125g of sushi rice over it, leaving a 1cm border at the top free of rice (see photographs on page 89). Be careful not to press too hard as this may ruin the rice.

Lay two pieces of fried salmon skin across the middle of the rice and top with a quarter each of the spring onions and mizuna leaves. Arrange the filling so that some of both the salmon skin and mizuna stick out at each end.

Hold the filling in place with your index fingers and roll the nori sheet over to make a cylinder and seal the roll with the tab of uncovered nori. Use the slats of the rolling mat to square up the roll and set aside to rest for a few minutes. Repeat with the remaining ingredients.

Cut each roll into eight pieces and arrange on a serving plate with wasabi, pickled ginger and soy sauce.

# power lunch with edamame, wakame and tuna

serves ● ● ● ●

This is sushi for people on the go – I often reach for it myself if there is a busy afternoon ahead. The brown rice has complex carbs that release energy slowly into the bloodstream. Wakame is said to be good for the metabolism and cleanses the blood – the effect is thought to be doubled when it is served with a salad dressing made with healthy oil. To cook the wholegrain rice you need to briefly forget everything you have learned about sushi rice as it demands totally different treatment.

# power lunch with edamame, wakame and tuna

300g frozen edamame

20g dried wakame

300g sashimi-grade tuna

1 green-skinned avocado, peeled and sliced

100g ikura (salmon eggs)

1 punnet shiso cress

small handful of coriander leaves

**for the brown sushi rice mixture (makes about 640g)**

300g long-grain brown rice

2 tablespoons poppy seeds

4 teaspoons extra virgin olive oil

4 teaspoons sushi vinegar

10g chives, finely chopped

sea salt and pepper

**to serve**

Japanese Vinaigrette (see page 42)

To cook the brown rice: first make a note of its volume in a measuring jug. Rinse the rice thoroughly under the tap and place in a heavy-bottomed saucepan. Add enough water to give 150 per cent of the volume of rice. Bring to the boil, cover and cook for 40 minutes over a low heat. Then remove the pan from the heat and set aside, still covered, for another 20 minutes.

Place the hot cooked rice in a bowl with the poppy seeds, olive oil, sushi vinegar and chives. Mix gently, then season with salt and pepper. Cover the bowl and leave to rest for 1 hour, or until the rice has cooled to room temperature.

Meanwhile, bring a kettle of water to the boil. Place the edamame in a heatproof bowl and cover with the hot water from the kettle. Leave to stand for 5 minutes, then drain and pod the beans.

Place the wakame in a small bowl and cover with cold water. Leave to rehydrate for 10 minutes, then drain.

Slice the tuna diagonally into 20 sashimi-style pieces, referring to the pictures on page 19 if necessary.

Divide the rice mixture among four noodle bowls or other large serving dishes. Top with the tuna sashimi, sliced avocado, wakame, salmon eggs and edamame. Garnish with shiso cress and coriander leaves and serve with a little dish of the Japanese vinaigrette.

Tip: in general this dish will work with any Japanese ingredients that take your fancy. You can also use fresh salmon, or a tartar mixture that uses up tuna trimmings from other recipes (see page 29).

# salmon, rocket and pesto maki

makes

Peppery rocket complements salmon in any sushi roll, whether it's made with brown or white rice. This roll is a good way to use salmon off-cuts and is eternally popular.

500g Prepared Brown Sushi Rice
   (see opposite)
50ml Feng Pesto (see page 44)
150g sashimi-grade salmon
4 sheets nori
60g rocket

**to serve**
wasabi, pickled ginger and soy sauce

Cook the brown rice following the recipe on page 96. Meanwhile, if you have not already done so, prepare the pesto as described on page 44 and decant into a squeeze bottle. Trim the salmon, discarding any brown bits.

Trim each sheet of nori down by one-fifth. Place one sheet on a bamboo rolling mat shiny side down and spread about 125g of brown rice over it, leaving a 1cm border at the top free of rice (see pictures on page 89).

Place a row of salmon along the middle of the rice. Top with a line pesto and about a quarter of the rocket leaves. Hold the filling in place with your index fingers and roll the nori over to make a cylinder, sealing the roll with the tab of uncovered nori. Use the slats of the rolling mat to square up the roll and set aside to rest for a few minutes. Repeat with the remaining ingredients.

Cut each roll into six pieces, discarding the ragged ends. Arrange the maki on a plate and serve with wasabi, pickled ginger and soy sauce.

# yellowtail and thai asparagus maki

makes

Here is an opportunity to use the off-cuts from other yellowtail dishes in this book. The rich, fatty fish works well with wholesome brown rice.

500g Prepared Brown Sushi Rice
  (see page 96)
16 spears Thai asparagus
salt
160g sashimi-grade yellowtail
4 sheets nori

**to serve**
wasabi, pickled ginger and soy sauce

Prepare the brown rice mixture following the recipe on page 96. While it is cooking, bring a kettle of water to the boil. Place the asparagus in a heatproof bowl. Cover with hot water from the kettle, add a little salt and set aside for a few minutes. Drain then plunge into ice-cold water to stop the cooking and help retain the colour.

Cut the yellowtail into small pieces.

Trim each sheet of nori down by one-fifth. Place one sheet on a rolling mat shiny side down and spread about 125g of brown rice over it, leaving a 1cm border at the top free of rice (see techniques on page 89).

Place a row of yellowtail along the middle of the rice and top with four spears of asparagus. Hold the filling in place with your index fingers and roll the nori over to make a cylinder, sealing the roll with the tab of uncovered nori. Use the slats of the rolling mat to help square up the roll and set aside to rest for a few minutes. Repeat with the remaining ingredients.

Cut each roll into six, discarding the ragged ends. Serve with wasabi, pickled ginger and soy sauce.

# avocado, chive and sesame maki

makes

This vegetarian option for brown rice maki is simple and tasty.

500g Prepared Brown Sushi Rice
   (see page 96)
1 green-skinned avocado
4 sheets nori
20 long chives
80g sesame seeds

**to serve**
wasabi, pickled ginger and soy sauce

First prepare the brown rice mixtrue as described on page 96. Meanwhile, quarter the avocado, peel off the skin, then cut each piece to give two wedges.

Trim each sheet of nori down by one-fifth. Place one sheet on a rolling mat shiny side down and spread about 125g of brown rice over it, leaving a 1cm border at the top free of rice (see techniques on page 89).

Lay two wedges of avocado along the middle of the rice. Top with five chives and a sprinkling of sesame seeds.

Hold the filling in place with your index fingers and roll the nori over to make a cylinder, sealing the roll with the tab of uncovered nori. Use the slats of the rolling mat to square up the roll and set aside to rest for a few minutes. Repeat with the remaining ingredients.

Cut each roll into six pieces, discarding the ragged ends, and arrange on a plate. Serve with the wasabi, pickled ginger and soy sauce.

# rolling inside-out maki

1. Trim each sheet of nori down by cutting a 3.5cm strip along the longest side to give a sheet measuring 15.5 x 20.5cm. Save the off-cuts for making gunkan nigiri and nori belts. Lay your first sheet of nori shiny-side down on a rolling mat and position it so that is close to you, near the edge of the work surface.

2. When the cooked sushi rice has reached a temperature of 28°C, gently spread about 150g of it over the nori, covering the whole sheet. Be careful not to press too hard as this may spoil the texture of the rice. Sprinkle the sesame seeds, or whatever mixture you are using to decorate the outside of the maki, evenly over the rice.

3. Quickly turn the square over so that the nori is uppermost. Arrange your chosen fillings across the middle of the nori.

4. Using your thumbs to lift the bamboo mat and your index fingers to hold the filling in place, roll the sushi up and over to form a neat cylinder. Seal the roll by tucking the top edge of the nori under the bottom edge – be sure to do this tightly so that the roll stays closed.

5. Press the bamboo slats of the rolling mat along the sides of the roll to shape it into a neat, square-sided maki. Set aside to rest for a few minutes.

6. Remove the roll from the bamboo mat. Use a sharp knife to trim off the rough ends, then cut each maki into eight pieces.

# inside-out maki with crushed wasabi peas

makes

This maki came about by accident while I was teaching a sushi course in Denmark. It was the day after a public holiday and I could not find any decent fresh fish for love or money, so I devised this very tasty vegetarian sushi. Wasabi peas are dried peas coated in a wasabi-flavoured crust. Normally eaten as a snack, they are widely available in Asian stores.

600g Prepared Sushi Rice (see page 15)
50ml Feng Pesto (see page 44)
4 spears green asparagus
1 green-skinned avocado
100g wasabi peas
100g black sesame seeds, toasted
4 sheets nori
24 long chives
50g mizuna leaves
50g rocket leaves

**to serve**
wasabi, pickled ginger and soy sauce

Cook the sushi rice as described on page 15. Meanwhile, make the pesto using the recipe on page 44.

Blanch the asparagus in a pot of boiling salted water for 4 minutes, then drain and plunge into ice-cold water. Once cool, halve each spear down the middle.

Quarter and peel the avocado, then cut each piece into three wedges. Use a food processor to crush the wasabi peas coarsely, then mix them with the black sesame seeds.

Trim each sheet of nori down by one-fifth. Place one sheet on a rolling mat and spread 150g of sushi rice over it (see page 100). Sprinkle the sesame-wasabi mixture over the rice, then flick the square over so that the nori is uppermost.

Arrange the filling across the middle of the nori: lay two pieces of asparagus and six chives so that the ends stick out either side; add a line of pesto, three avocado wedges, a small handful of mizuna and a small handful of rocket.

Roll the maki tightly and seal by tucking the top end of the nori under the bottom end. Use the rolling mat to square up the maki and set it aside to rest for a few minutes while you repeat with the remaining ingredients.

Cut each roll into eight, arrange on a plate and serve with the wasabi, pickled ginger and soy sauce.

# california sunset inside-out maki with crab and tobiko

makes

Globally, this is the most famous maki, but all too often made with crabsticks. Even in Japan some sushi bars will use them, which is strange as they come from large processing factories and are made from a dubious mix of white fish leftovers and artificial flavouring. For a real treat I recommend high quality picked crab claw meat. Yuzu-flavoured tobiko is optional in this recipe: wasabi or plum varieties would work as well.

600g Prepared Sushi Rice (see page 15)
50ml Feng Mayo (see page 44)
1 cucumber
1 green-skinned avocado
160g white crabmeat
4 sheets nori
100g mixed black and white sesame seeds
60g yuzu tobiko

**to serve**
wasabi, pickled ginger and soy sauce

Cook the sushi rice following the method on page 15. Meanwhile, prepare the mayo as described on page 44.

Cut the cucumber lengthways down the middle and set one half aside for use in other dishes. Use a spoon to scrape out the seeds, then cut the cucumber into four long sticks.

Quarter and peel the avocado, then cut each piece into three wedges. Carefully pick through the crabmeat, removing any shell or cartilage.

Trim each sheet of nori down by one-fifth. Place one sheet on a rolling mat and spread about 150g of sushi rice over it, covering the whole sheet (see page 100). Sprinkle the sesame seeds and tobiko over the rice, then flick the square over so that the black seaweed side is uppermost.

Arrange the filling across the middle of the nori: one cucumber stick, a line of mayo, three pieces of avocado and a quarter of the crabmeat.

Roll the maki tightly and seal by tucking the top end of the nori under the bottom end. Square up the sides and set aside to rest while you repeat with the remaining ingredients.

Cut each roll into eight pieces, discarding the ragged ends, and serve with the wasabi, pickled ginger and soy sauce.

# vegetarian inside-out maki with pickles

makes ● ● ● ● ● ● ● ●
● ● ● ● ● ● ● ●
● ● ● ● ● ● ● ●
● ● ● ● ● ● ● ●

Most Japanese pickles will work in this recipe. Try sakurazuke (pink pickled mooli), takuwantoro (yellow pickled mooli), shibazuke (purple pickled aubergine), and kappa (Asian pickled cucumber), just to name a few of the possibilties.

600g Prepared Sushi Rice (see page 15)

1 cucumber

1 green-skinned avocado

4 sheets nori

100g mixed black and white sesame seeds

20 long chives

120g Japanese pickles, drained

**to serve**
wasabi, pickled ginger and soy sauce

Cook the sushi rice following the method on page 15.

Cut the cucumber lengthways down the middle and set one half aside for use in other dishes. Use a spoon to scrape out the seeds, then cut the cucumber into four long sticks.

Quarter and peel the avocado, then cut each piece into three wedges.

Trim each sheet of nori down by one-fifth. Place one sheet on a rolling mat and spread about 150g of sushi rice over it, covering the whole sheet (see page 100). Sprinkle the sesame seeds over the rice, then flick the square over so that the black seaweed side is uppermost.

Arrange the filling across the middle of the nori: one cucumber stick, three pieces of avocado, five chives and a quarter of the Japanese pickles.

Roll the maki tightly and seal by tucking the top end of the nori under the bottom end. Square up the sides and set aside to rest for a few minutes while you repeat the process with the remaining ingredients.

Cut each roll into eight pieces, discarding the ragged ends. Arrange the sushi on a plate and serve with the wasabi, pickled ginger and soy sauce.

# san fran rainbow roll

makes

500g Prepared Sushi Rice (see page 15)
160g salmon sashimi block
160g tuna sashimi block
1 cucumber
4 sheets nori
20-40 long chives
120g sashimi-grade yellowtail off-cuts,
    finely chopped

**to serve**
wasabi, pickled ginger and soy sauce

First prepare the sushi rice following the method on page 15. Meanwhile, cut the salmon and tuna into 12 nigiri slices each (see the pictures on pages 19 and 26).

Cut the cucumber lengthways down the middle and set one half aside for use in other dishes. Use a spoon to scrape out the seeds, then cut the cucumber into four long sticks.

Trim each sheet of nori down by one-fifth. Place one sheet on a rolling mat shiny side down and spread about 125g of sushi rice over it, leaving a 1cm border at the top free of rice (see techniques on page 100).

Lay six of the nigiri slices, alternating the salmon and tuna, along the bottom half of the rice. Flick the whole square over so that the nori is uppermost.

Arrange the filling across the middle of the nori: one cucumber stick, 5-10 chives and a quarter of the yellowtail.

Roll the maki tightly into a cylinder and seal with the tab of uncovered nori. Use the slats of the rolling mat to square up the maki and leave to rest for a few minutes. Repeat with the remaining ingredients.

Cut each roll into eight pieces, discarding the ragged ends, and arrange on a plate. Serve with the wasabi, pickled ginger and soy sauce.

# gravadlax with salmon, rocket and pesto

makes

Gravadlax needs eight to ten days to cure, so bear this in mind when you are planning to make this dish. Alternatively, you can use ready-made traditional dill gravadlax, or smoked salmon, making sure that each slice is only a few millimetres thick.

500g Prepared Sushi Rice (see page 15)

50ml Feng Pesto (see page 44)

4 sheets nori

320g gravadlax (see page 67)

120g sashimi-grade salmon off-cuts, finely chopped

50g rocket leaves

**to serve**

wasabi, pickled ginger and soy sauce

Cook the sushi rice according to the instructions on page 15. Meanwhile, prepare the pesto following the recipe on page 44 and place in a squeeze bottle. Cut the gravadlax into 24 nigiri slices following the technique on page 19.

Trim each sheet of nori down by one-fifth. Place one sheet on a rolling mat shiny side down and spread about 125g of sushi rice over it, leaving a 1cm border at the top free of rice (see page 100).

Lay six nigiri slices along the bottom half of the rice. Flick the whole square over so that the nori is uppermost.

Arrange the filling along the centre of the nori: a line of pesto, a quarter of the salmon and a handful of rocket.

Holding the filling in place with your index fingers, roll up into a cylinder and seal the maki with the tab of uncovered nori. Square up the sides of the maki and leave to rest for a few minutes. Repeat with the remaining ingredients.

Cut each roll into eight pieces, discarding the ragged ends. Arrange on a plate and serve with the wasabi, pickled ginger and soy sauce.

# organic roast beef with horseradish cream, chives and cucumber

makes

Here is the maki version of my beef nigiri. It is a good option if you want to make something quick for a drinks party. Buy ready-roast organic beef that is nicely pink in the middle, and have the butcher cut each slice no more than a few millimetres thick.

500g Prepared Sushi Rice (see page 15)

100ml Fresh Horseradish and Wasabi Cream (see page 74)

1 cucumber

4 sheets nori

400g organic roast beef, about 20 slices

20 long chives

**to serve**

wasabi, pickled ginger and soy sauce

Cook the sushi rice according to the instructions on page 15. Meanwhile, prepare the horseradish and wasabi cream following the recipe on page 74.

Cut the cucumber lengthways down the middle and set one half aside for use in other dishes. Use a spoon to scrape out the seeds, then cut the cucumber into four long sticks.

Trim each sheet of nori down by one-fifth. Place one sheet on a rolling mat shiny side down and spread about 125g of sushi rice over it, leaving a 1cm border at the top free of rice (see techniques on page 100).

Lay five slices of beef so that they overlap along the bottom half of the rice. Flick the whole square over so that the nori is uppermost. Arrange the filling across the middle of the nori: a generous spread of horseradish and wasabi cream, one cucumber stick and five chives.

Roll tightly up into a cylinder and seal the maki with the tab of uncovered nori. Use slats of the rolling mat to square up the sides and leave to rest for a few minutes. Repeat with the remaining ingredients.

Cut each roll into eight pieces, discarding the ragged ends. Arrange on a plate and serve with the wasabi, pickled ginger and soy sauce.

# tamago roll with roast bell pepper salsa

makes

On one hand this maki is designed to impress; on the other it's a cost-effective vegetarian sushi roll. Use a large tamago pan if possible, otherwise cook the tamago in a large non-stick frying pan and cut the individual sheets of omelette to size.

500g Prepared Sushi Rice (see page 15)
4 sheets nori
100g cream cheese
80 long chives

**for the tamago sheets**
6 organic eggs
2 teaspoons caster sugar
2 teaspoons mirin
2 teaspoons sake
pinch of salt
olive oil, for greasing

**for the salsa**
2 yellow bell peppers, roasted, deseeded and peeled
2 red bell peppers, roasted, deseeded and peeled
1 tablespoon red wine vinegar
1 tablespoon honey
$1/2$ teaspoon shichimi powder

**to serve**
wasabi, pickled ginger and soy sauce

Cook the sushi rice according to the instructions on page 15.

Prepare the tamago mixture following the techniques on pages 80-81. Cook as instructed, but instead of rolling the omelette, turn the individual sheets out onto a rolling mat as soon as they are set and leave them to cool.

For the salsa: finely dice the roast peppers and place in a bowl with the vinegar, honey and shichimi. Marinate for 5 minutes, then drain to remove the excess liquid.

Trim each sheet of nori down by one-fifth. Place one sheet on a rolling mat shiny side down and spread about 125g of sushi rice over it, leaving a 1cm border at the top free of rice (see techniques on page 100).

Lay a sheet of omelette on top of the rice. Flick the whole square over so that the nori is uppermost. Arrange the filling across the middle of the nori: a generous spread of cream cheese, 3 tablespoons salsa and 20 long chives.

Roll the maki tightly into a cylinder and seal by tucking the top end of nori under the bottom end. Square up the sides and leave to rest for a few minutes while you repeat the process with the remaining ingredients.

Cut each roll into eight pieces, discarding the ragged ends. Arrange them on a plate and serve with the wasabi, pickled ginger and soy sauce.

# rolling temaki

Temaki are cone-shaped hand rolls traditionally eaten at the sushi counter as quickly as the sushi chef can produce them. They are also a perfect party piece. Invite your friends to make their own – all you need to do is prepare the ingredients and show them how. Any maki filling is suitable for temaki.

1. Cut the nori straight down the middle, so that each sheet gives two rectangular pieces. Lay the first sheet of nori shiny-side down on the work surface. Place 50g of cooked sushi rice in a round, flat circle on the left side of the nori. Then stick 2-3 rice grains in the bottom right-hand corner of the nori to help seal the temaki later.

2. Smear a dab of wasabi in the centre of the circle of rice.

3. Lay your chosen filling diagonally across the middle of the rice so that it sticks out at the top left-hand corner.

4. Lift the bottom left-hand bottom corner of the nori up and across the filling, rolling the temaki over into a cone.

5. Use the rice that you previously stuck in the bottom right-hand corner to seal the nori.

6. Hand the finished temaki straight to your guests, or place on a serving plate, and repeat the process with the remaining ingredients.

# green temaki

makes ∷ ∷

400g Prepared Sushi Rice (see page 15)
1 green-skinned avocado
4 sheets nori
50g mizuna leaves
20-40 long chives
80g kappa or other Japanese pickles

**to serve**
wasabi, pickled ginger and soy sauce

Cook the sushi rice according to the instructions on page 15. Meanwhile, quarter and peel the avocado, then cut each wedge into two pieces.

Cut the nori straight down the middle, so you have eight half sheets in total. Lay one sheet of nori shiny-side down on a work surface and place 50g of cooled sushi rice in a round, flat circle on the left side. Stick 2-3 rice grains in the right bottom corner, to help seal the temaki later.

For each temaki use a handful of mizuna leaves, a wedge of avocado, some chives and one-eighth of the pickles and place the filling in the middle of the rice so that it sticks out at the top left-hand corner.

Lift the bottom left-hand bottom corner and roll the temaki into a cone using the rice in the bottom right-hand corner to seal the nori. Repeat with the remaining ingredients and serve with wasabi, pickled ginger and soy sauce.

# yellowtail temaki with rocket, shiso and feng mayo

makes ∷∷

400g Prepared Sushi Rice (see page 15)
50ml Feng Mayo (see page 44)
4 sheets nori
50g rocket leaves
16 nigiri slices yellowtail
1 punnet shiso cress

**to serve**
wasabi, pickled ginger and soy sauce

Cook the sushi rice according to the instructions on page 15. Meanwhile, if you have not already done so, make the Feng Mayo and place in a squeeze bottle.

Cut the nori straight down the middle, so you have eight half sheets in total. Lay one sheet of nori shiny-side down on a work surface and place 50g of the cooled sushi rice in a round, flat circle on the left side. Stick 2-3 rice grains in the right bottom corner, to help seal the temaki later.

Place the filling in the middle of the rice so that it sticks out at the top left-hand corner. First a generous dot of mayo, then one-eighth of the rocket leaves, two slices of yellowtail nigiri and a cluster of shiso cress.

Lift the bottom left-hand bottom corner and roll the temaki into a cone using the rice in the bottom right-hand corner to seal the nori. Repeat with the remaining ingredients and serve with wasabi, pickled ginger and soy sauce.

# tempura

Tempura is vegetables or fish coated with a light batter and deep-fried. Some believe the idea arrived in Japan with the Portuguese in the mid-15th century. A hundred years later tempura of sea bream wrapped in shiso leaf had become a very exclusive dish. Later the technique spread to street food stalls, where busy workers would pick up tempura for a quick bite. In Japan there are restaurants specialising in tempura. The most prestigious use pure untoasted sesame oil for frying, while cheaper establishments will use lesser quality toasted sesame oil mixed with a high proportion of other oils such as soya or corn oil. I like to use sunflower oil as it seems to give a lighter result.

Pesto tiger prawn tempura

# making tempura

When it comes to deep-fried food, Western people tend to favour a golden batter, however Japanese tempura batter is paler in colour. To make 500ml of batter you will need 500ml of ice-cold water and 250g tempura flour (plus extra for dusting). Alternatively, start with 500ml of ice-cold water and whisk in 1 egg yolk, 40g cornflour and 250g self-raising flour.

1. Take your jug of ice-cold water and add the flour to the water. Never add the water to the flour.

2. Gently whisk the ingredients together so that the batter has the consistency of double cream with lots of little lumps of flour in it. The air bubbles and lumps of flour will help make the tempura crisp – as will placing the batter in the fridge for 30 minutes to set and chill.

3. Dust all the ingredients in tempura flour. This will ensure an even coating of batter.

4. Heat the oil to 180°C in a heavy wok or deep-fryer. Remove the cold batter from the fridge and dip the ingredients in it. Use tongs to transfer each piece quickly to the hot oil, gently moving the tempura back and forwards in the oil before letting it go to stop it dropping to the base of the pan.

5. Never fry more than six pieces of tempura at a time. This ensures that the temperature of the oil does not drop significantly when you add the ingredients, which would make the tempura absorb some of the oil and take too long to fry. It also helps prevent the tempura sticking together.

6. Leave the cooked tempura to drain on sheets of paper towel, then season with sea salt before serving.

Highly seasoned dipping sauces such as the two recipes here enhance the taste of tempura and help cut through the fattiness of the deep-fried batter. Other condiments commonly served alongside tempura are shown below. Grated mooli is particularly important as it aids digestion.

Kimchee base

Shichimi powder

Chopped pickled ginger

Chilli oil

Thai sweet chilli sauce

# dipping sauces and garnishes

## basic tempura dipping sauce
makes about 550ml

250ml soy sauce

250ml boiling water

2 tablespoons dashi powder

2 tablespoons caster sugar

1 tablespoon finely chopped ginger

½ teaspoon shichimi powder

Combine all the ingredients in a large measuring jug. Pour into a squeeze bottle and store in the fridge, where it will keep for up to 2 weeks.

## vegetarian dipping sauce
makes about 550ml

250ml soy sauce

250ml boiling water

2 tablespoons good quality vegetarian stock

2 tablespoons caster sugar

1 tablespoon finely chopped pickled ginger

2 tablespoons mixed black and white sesame seeds

Combine all the ingredients in a large measuring jug. Pour into a squeeze bottle and store in the fridge, where it will keep for up to 2 weeks.

Finely grated mooli

Sea salt

Basic tempura dipping sauce

Vegetarian dipping sauce

# vegetarian tempura

serves ● ● ● ●

Making a batch of vegetarian tempura is the perfect opportunity to master the technique before moving on to more pricey ingredients such as fish. In principle, any vegetable can be fried in tempura batter; this recipe contains some of my favourites.

500ml Basic Tempura Batter
(see page 118)

1 beetroot

1 yellow beetroot

$^1/_4$ butternut squash

2 large fresh shitake mushrooms

4 oyster mushrooms

2 baby aubergines

1 small courgette

1 small mild pepper, such as
sweet romano

2 litres sunflower oil, for deep-frying

tempura flour, for dusting

sea salt

**to serve**

400g Prepared Sushi Rice (see page 15)

4 teaspoons toasted sesame seeds

200ml Vegetarian Dipping Sauce
(see page 121)

100g mooli, finely grated

Make the tempura batter according to the recipe on page 118 and place in the fridge to chill.

The vegetables need to be cut into pieces of similar size so that they will cook evenly. Do not peel the beetroot or butternut squash, simply cut them into discs $^1/_2$cm thick.

Trim the base off the shitake mushrooms, then cut them in half leaving the stalk attached. The oyster mushrooms can be left whole. Halve the baby aubergines, but leave the stalks intact (these are not edible but look attractive). Cut the courgette and pepper diagonally into ovals $^1/_2$cm thick.

Heat the sunflower oil to 180°C in a deep-fryer or large heavy-based saucepan. Place the tempura flour in a bowl and remove the cold batter from the fridge. Working with one variety at a time, dust the vegetables with tempura flour then dip in the batter. Fry the root vegetables and aubergine for $2^1/_2$-3 minutes, and the peppers, courgette and both varieties of mushroom for $1^1/_2$ minutes.

Remove the cooked tempura to a tray lined with kitchen paper to drain. Season with salt.

Divide the cooked sushi rice into four portions and shape them into a triangle using an onigiri mould, or use another tool such as a round cutter. Place a portion of rice on each serving plate, garnish with sesame seeds and stack the tempura vegetables around the rice. Serve immediately with the dipping sauce and grated mooli.

chilli tuna tempura

salmon, dill and tobiko tempura

# chilli tuna tempura

makes ● ● ● ●

Adding extra crunch or flavour to tempura batter makes a brilliant variation. The following recipe is perfect served as a snack with cold beer on a hot day.

250ml Basic Tempura Batter
  (see page 118)
1 tablespoon kimchee base
1 tablespoon shichimi powder
2 litres sunflower oil, for deep-frying
150g tuna sashimi block
tempura flour, for dusting
sea salt

**to serve**
100ml Thai sweet chilli sauce

Make a half quantity of the basic tempura batter on page 118, adding the kimchee base and shichimi powder to the flour. Put the batter in the fridge to rest and chill.

Heat the sunflower oil in a deep-fryer or heavy based saucepan to 180°C. Cut the tuna loin into 12 pieces approximately 1cm thick and turn them lightly in the flour.

When the oil is ready, dip the tuna in the cold batter and, working with six pieces at a time, fry for about 2 minutes, or until light golden. Transfer the cooked tempura to a tray lined with kitchen paper to drain. Season with sea salt and serve with the Thai sweet chilli sauce.

## salmon, dill and tobiko tempura

This is my Scandinavian take on tempura. Follow the recipe above but instead of adding the kimchee base and shichimi to the tempura batter, gently stir in 25g finely chopped dill and 2 tablespoons yuzu tobiko just before you put the batter in the fridge to chill. Replace the tuna with salmon sashimi and serve the cooked tempura with 100ml Scandia Dill Dressing (see page 43).

# pesto tiger prawn tempura

makes ● ● ● ●
● ● ● ●
● ● ● ●

Here is a very refreshing Italian twist on tempura.

50ml Feng Pesto (see page 44)
250ml Basic Tempura Batter
  (see page 118)
2 litres sunflower oil, for deep-frying
12 raw tiger prawns, size 16/20
tempura flour, for dusting
sea salt

**to serve**
100ml Basic Tempura Dipping Sauce
  (see page 121)

First make the Feng Pesto and Basic Tempura Dipping Sauce according to their respective recipes. Transfer both to squeeze bottles.

Take a half quantity of the Basic Tempura Batter on page 118 and stir in 50ml of the pesto so that it is evenly distributed. Place the batter in the fridge to chill.

Heat the sunflower oil in a deep-fryer or heavy-based saucepan to 180°C. Meanwhile, peel prawns: twist off the heads, remove the jackets but leave the tails on. Slit along the backs and lift out the intestines. Rinse the prawns, pat dry with kitchen paper, then turn them lightly in the flour.

When the oil is ready, dip each prawn in the batter and fry in the hot oil for about 2 minutes, or until light golden. Do not cook more than six prawns at a time. Transfer the cooked tempura to a tray lined with kitchen paper to drain. Season with sea salt and serve with the dipping sauce.

Tip: when frying tiger prawns, carefully hold them by the tail end, keeping your hands clear of the hot oil, and move the prawns back and forth in the oil a few times to help make the tempura large and crisp.

# extra-crunchy baby squid tempura with pickled cucumber

serves ● ● ● ●

Cornmeal provides the extra crunch to this tempura. The cucumber salad is a take on my grandma's old recipe which she always served with whole roasted chicken and new potatoes. But here you go – it has found its way into my Japanese cuisine.

500ml Basic Tempura Batter
  (see page 118)
100g cornmeal
$1/2$ tablespoon shichimi powder
12 baby squid
2 litres sunflower oil, for deep-frying
sea salt

**for the pickled cucumber**
10cm piece dried kelp
200ml sushi vinegar
100g caster sugar
1 cucumber

To start the cucumber salad, rinse the kelp under the tap, then place in a saucepan with the vinegar and sugar. Heat the mixture until it just reaches boiling point, then remove from the heat and set aside to cool.

Make the basic tempura batter according to the recipe on page 118, adding the cornmeal and shichimi to the flour and an extra 100ml cold water to the jug. Chill thoroughly.

To continue the cucumber salad: finely slice the cucumber on a Japanese mandolin then place in a mixing bowl. Lift the kelp from the vinegar mixture and pour the liquid over the cucumber. Leave to marinate for at least 30 minutes.

Working under running tap water, remove the hard membrane from each squid body (this looks like a piece of plastic). Use your index finger to remove any soft tissue or slime from inside the body. With a pair of scissors, cut between the eyes and squid head, detaching the tentacles. Discard the eyes and any slimy bits. Cut each squid body into three pieces. Rinse everything once more in cold water and pat dry with kitchen paper. Set aside in a bowl.

Heat the sunflower oil in a deep-fryer or heavy-based saucepan to 180°C. Turn the baby squid in the flour, then dip in the batter. Fry six pieces of the squid at a time for approximately 2 minutes, or until light golden.

Transfer the cooked tempura to a tray lined with kitchen paper to drain. Season with sea salt and serve with the pickled cucumber salad.

# magic's coconut tempura prawns with mango and papaya salsa

serves ● ● ● ●

Here is my fiancé David's Caribbean version of tempura. We often serve it as a nibble on hot summer days while guests are waiting for the real party pieces to come off the barbecue.

500ml Basic Tempura Batter
  (see page 118)
12 raw tiger prawns, size 16/20
2 litres vegetable oil, for deep-frying
tempura flour, for dusting
70g unsweetened desiccated coconut

**for the mango and papaya salsa**
1 large ripe mango
1 large ripe papaya
1 red onion, finely sliced
juice of 2 limes
3 tablespoons red wine vinegar
3 tablespoons caster sugar

First make the salsa: peel and deseed the mango and papaya, cutting the flesh into 1cm cubes. Combine the fruit in a mixing bowl with the red onion, lime juice, red wine vinegar and caster sugar and stir gently. Cover and place the salsa in the fridge to chill for at least 30 minutes.

Make the basic tempura batter according to the recipe on page 118 and leave it to rest in the fridge.

Remove the heads and jackets from the prawns, but leave the tails intact. Slit each prawn along its back and lift out the intestinal thread.

Heat the oil to 180°C in a deep-fryer or heavy-based saucepan. Place the flour and desiccated coconut in separate dishes. Remove the cold batter from the fridge.

Working one at a time, dust the prawns in the flour, dip in the batter, then roll the coated prawns in coconut before placing in the hot oil. Fry for 2 minutes or until light golden.

Transfer the cooked tempura to a tray lined with kitchen paper to drain briefly, then serve immediately with the mango and papaya salsa.

# japanese-style fish and chips with cod and rémoulade

serves ● ● ● ●

This is my most ambitious fusion – Japan meets Britain with a Danish detour. The Danish influence is the tradition of serving fish and chips with rémoulade sauce; something that was totally forbidden me in my childhood and is unapologetically central to my Feng Sushi recipe. I console myself with the fact that a homemade rémoulade bears little or no resemblance to the store-bought stuff. Plus I use sweet potatoes instead of some of the starchy whites for the chips, so it's as near as you can get to a sin-free treat and something that no parent should feel bad about serving to children... occasionally...

The quantity of pickled vegetables in this recipe is much more than you'll need for one batch of rémoulade sauce, but it's the sort of thing that is impractical to make in smaller amounts. The vegetables keep well in their cooled pickling liquid in a tightly sealed jar in the fridge, and you can use them as an accompaniment to many other things. I use sustainable Icelandic cod for this dish but monkfish tail also works well.

# japanese-style fish and chips with cod and rémoulade

1 fillet cod, about 600-700g, skinned

2 large sweet potatoes

2 large Maris Piper potatoes

3 litres sunflower oil, for deep-frying

**for the pickles**

2 large carrots

2 large courgette

400g cauliflower

400g broccoli

400g celery

400g butternut squash

300g caster sugar

small handful of whole black peppercorns

1 tablespoon mild curry powder

1 tablespoon turmeric

1 piece of kombu, or 1 bay leaf

sushi vinegar

3-4 tablespoons cornflour

**for the rémoulade sauce**

1 whole egg

2 egg yolks

4 teaspoons yuzu juice

4 teaspoons sushi vinegar

1 tablespoon caster sugar

100ml olive oil

200ml vegetable oil

200ml sweet chilli sauce

salt and pepper

To make the pickles: peel and cut all the vegetables into 1cm dice. Place in a large heavy-based saucepan with the sugar, spices and kombu. Add enough sushi vinegar to cover the vegetables completely. Bring to the boil and cook until the vegetables are cooked but still very crunchy.

Place a large colander on top of a large bowl and drain the vegetables, saving the liquid. Return all the liquid to the saucepan and bring it back to the boil. Dissolve the cornflour in a little cold water and gradually add it to the vinegar mixture to give a thick, smooth consistency (you may not need to use all the cornflour). Pour the sauce over the pickled vegetables, stir, and set aside to cool.

To make the rémoulade sauce: place the egg, yolks, yuzu juice, sushi vinegar and caster sugar in a food processor and blend until white and fluffy. Combine the two oils and add them to the mixture gradually, blending to give an even consistency, then pour in the sweet chilli sauce.

Take a quantity of pickled vegetables similar to the total volume of sauce and add it to the food processor. Pulse the mixture just enough to give a coarse, lumpy dipping sauce. Season to taste with pepper, salt and sugar.

Prepare the tempura batter: start with a jug of iced water and gradually add the combined flours until the mixture is lumpy and airy. Place in the fridge to chill.

**for the batter**
1 litre ice-cold water
400g Japanese tempura flour
100g plain flour
tempura flour, for dusting

Rinse the fish and pat dry with kitchen paper. Place the cod on a board and cut the fillet down the middle, following the line of the backbone. Trim off any flabby bits and discard. Cut the fillet diagonally into 1cm thick slices, working at a 45-degree angle so that each piece is cut on the bias. You should aim to have 16-18 pieces.

Cut both varieties of potatoes into chips. Keeping the batches separate, rinse them in cold water and leave to drain in a colander. Heat the oil to 180°C in a deep-fryer or large heavy-based saucepan. When the oil is ready, fry the Maris Piper potatoes for 2 minutes, then add the sweet potatoes and continue frying for a further 8 minutes. Drain the chips on kitchen paper and season with salt.

Dust the cod slices in flour, then dip them in the chilled tempura batter. Fry for 2-3 minutes or until light golden, then drain on kitchen paper and season with salt and pepper. Stack the chips on a serving plate, place the cod on top and drizzle with the rémoulade sauce before serving.

## sushi with tempura

Sushi with tempura is the perfect balance of naughty and nice. Adding
just a few pieces of crispy tempura to a maki roll or temaki gives the
maximum effect without piling on the calories. These rolls are good to
share, and when served in combination with other dishes allow you to
enjoy flavourful deep-fried food while still keeping the meal lean.

# shitake mushroom roll with chives and teriyaki sauce

makes

Shitake mushrooms, a good source of antioxidants, are categorised as a umami ingredient, foods with the 'fifth taste' that is found so often in Japanese cuisine. This inside-out maki roll with a deep-fried filling has plenty of flavour and texture.

4 teaspoons Simple Teriyaki Sauce
  (see page 44)

280g Prepared Sushi Rice (see page 15)

250ml Basic Tempura Batter
  (see page 118)

6 fresh shitake mushrooms

2 litres sunflower oil, for deep-frying

tempura flour, for dusting

2 sheets nori

50g mixed black and white sesame seeds

1 punnet shiso cress, leaves picked, some
  reserved for granish

10-20 long chives

**to serve**

grated mooli, wasabi paste, pickled ginger
  and soy sauce

If you have not already done so, make the teriyaki sauce as on page 44 and decant it into a squeeze bottle.

Cook the sushi rice as per the instructions on page 15 and, while the rice is boiling, make a half quantity of the tempura batter on page 118 and place in the fridge to rest.

Brush the shitake mushrooms clean with a pastry brush, trim away the base of the stalks, and cut the mushrooms in half lengthways leaving the stalk attached.

Heat the vegetable oil to 180°C in a deep-fryer or heavy based saucepan. Dust the shitake in flour, dip in the cold tempura batter, and fry for a few minutes until golden and crisp. Transfer the cooked tempura to a plate lined with kitchen paper to drain.

When the sushi rice is ready, roll into maki following the pictures on page 100 if necessary. Place a sheet of nori on a bamboo mat, spread 140g cooked sushi rice over the entire surface and sprinkle with the sesame seeds and most of the shiso cress. Flick the over the square so the seaweed is uppermost. In the middle of the maki, place a line of teriyaki sauce, shitake tempura and chives. Roll the maki tightly, sealing it by tucking the top end of the nori under bottom end. Repeat with the remaining ingredients.

Cut each roll into eight pieces, discarding the ends, garnish with the remaining shiso cress and serve with the traditional accompaniments.

# tiger prawn inside-out roll with thai asparagus and feng mayo

makes

This is a gorgeous maki roll, probably the second most popular maki in the Western sushi world – California maki having a strong first position.

280g Prepared Sushi Rice (see page 15)

250ml Basic Tempura Batter (see page 118)

4 teaspoons Feng Mayo (see page 44)

1 small punnet Thai asparagus

4 raw tiger prawns, size 16/20

2 litres sunflower oil, for deep-frying

tempura flour, for dusting

2 sheets nori

50g mixed black and white sesame seeds

**to serve**

grated mooli, wasabi paste, pickled ginger and soy sauce

Cook the sushi rice as per the instructions on page 15 and, while the rice is boiling, mix a half quantity of the tempura batter recipe on page 118 and leave it to rest in the fridge.

If you have not already done so, make the Feng Mayo as described on page 44 and place it in a squeeze bottle.

Bring a saucepan of salted water to the boil. Blanch the asparagus for 1 minute, then plunge it into ice-cold water.

Peel the tiger prawns, removing the intestinal threads, then rinse and pat dry. Skewer the prawns from belly to tail to stretch them out and make the maki easy to roll.

Heat the vegetable oil to 180°C in a deep-fryer or heavy-based saucepan. Dust the prawns in flour, dip in the tempura batter and fry for a few minutes until golden and crisp. Transfer to a plate lined with kitchen paper to drain, then remove the skewers from the prawns.

When the sushi rice is ready, roll the maki, referring to the pictures on page 100 as necessary. Place a sheet of nori on a bamboo mat, spread 140g cooked sushi rice over the surface and sprinkle all over with the sesame seeds. Flick the square over so the seaweed is uppermost. In the middle of the square place a row of mayonnaise, asparagus and tiger prawn tempura. Roll the maki tightly, closing it by tucking in top end of nori under bottom end.

Cut the roll in eight pieces, discarding the ends, and serve with the traditional accompaniments.

# tempura wild salmon temaki with ikura and yuzu tobiko

makes ::::

Wild salmon deserves its place in the sushi world; nonetheless I find it safest to eat this beautiful fish cooked. As you are already 'pushing the boat out' for this dish I recommend finishing it off in style with a few ikura and tobiko 'sea pearls'.

400g Prepared Sushi Rice (see page 15)

250ml Basic Tempura Batter
   (see page 118)

50ml Feng Mayo (see page 44)

80g wild salmon

2 litres sunflower oil, for deep-frying

tempura flour, for dusting

4 sheets nori

100g mizuna leaves

40g ikura (salmon eggs)

40g yuzu tobiko

**to serve**

grated mooli, wasabi paste, pickled ginger
   and soy sauce

Prepare the sushi rice following the instructions on page 15. While the rice is cooking, make a half quantity of the tempura batter recipe on page 118 and leave to rest in the fridge. If you have not already done so, make the Feng Mayo as described on page 44 and place it in a squeeze bottle.

Cut the salmon sashimi style into eight pieces following the pictures on page 19 if necessary.

Heat vegetable oil to 180°C in a deep-fryer or heavy-based saucepan. Dust the salmon in flour, dip in the cold tempura batter and fry for a few minutes until golden and crisp. Drain on a plate lined with kitchen paper.

Cut each sheet of nori in half to give a total of eight pieces. When the sushi rice has cooled, make temaki following the pictures on page 112 if necessary. Lay one sheet of nori shiny-side down and place 50g of the sushi rice in a round, flat circle on the left side. Stick 2-3 rice grains in the right bottom corner, to help seal the temaki later.

Place the filling in the middle of the rice so that it sticks out at the top left-hand corner: use one-eighth of the mizuna, one piece of wild salmon tempura and a dot of mayo per temaki. Lift the left hand bottom corner of the seaweed and roll the nori into a cone, using the rice grains to seal the nori. Repeat with the remaining ingredients.

Place the temaki in tall glasses and garnish them with the ikura and yuzu tobiko, then serve with the traditional sushi accompaniments.

Roberto, an old Mexican chef, first introduced me to this combination. He'd often make sushi as he knew it from his homeland for staff who were tired of the healthy Japanese version and craved something richer. We nicknamed it the 'triple bypass batter' for its rich cream cheese and double-frying technique, but I've reinvented it here in a leaner incarnation featuring tuna. This dish is still no saint, but it is delicious to share and has proved a stellar hit with Feng Sushi customers.

First prepare the sushi rice following the method on page 15. While the rice is cooking, make the tempura batter following the recipe on page 118 and leave to rest in the fridge. Cut the tuna into six pieces, no more than 1/2 cm thick but about 3cm in diameter.

Heat the vegetable oil to 180°C in a deep-fryer or heavy-based saucepan. Dust the tuna in the flour, then dip into the cold tempura batter and place in the hot oil. Fry for a few minutes until light golden. Set aside to drain on a plate lined with kitchen paper and sprinkle with sea salt. Remove the oil from the heat and set it aside, along with the remaining tempura batter.

Shape maki rolls referring to the pictures on page 89 as necessary. Spread half the cooled sushi rice over one sheet of nori. Spread generously with 40g cream cheese, 2 teaspoons kimchee base, half the chopped spring onion and three pieces of tuna tempura. Roll the maki very tightly – this will help it keep its shape while frying. Repeat the process to make a second roll.

Return the oil to 180°C. Cut each maki roll in half. Dust each piece in flour, dip in the remaining tempura batter and fry for 2 minutes. Drain briefly on kitchen paper, then carefully cut each maki roll into five pieces and serve them immediately with the traditional accompaniments.

240g Prepared Sushi Rice (see page 15)
500ml Basic Tempura Batter
  (see page 118)
100g yellowfin tuna
2 litres sunflower oil, for deep-frying
tempura flour, for dusting
sea salt
2 sheets nori
80g Philadelphia Lite cream cheese
4 teaspoons kimchee base
1 spring onion, finely chopped

**to serve**

grated mooli, wasabi paste, pickled
  ginger and soy sauce

# deep-fried
# tuna maki

makes

# east|west
## noodles and rice

There is nothing like Japanese noodles for simplicity: a few ingredients in a bowl and you have a magical meal. However I do think that efforts to reproduce authentic noodle dishes outside Japan often fail, so decided to take a different approach to the noodle section of Feng Sushi's menu. It became our playground. I was looking for soul food – nutritious dishes with deep flavours. Working with the chefs, we came up with a global tour de force, incorporating fine ingredients from various countries into Japanese cuisine.

Moroccan pumpkin ragout with soba noodle soup

**Spaghetti** this thin wheat pasta from Italy makes a reasonable substitute for Japanese wheat noodles, and is preferred for some fusion recipes.

**Soba noodles** in Japanese, soba means buckwheat as well as the noodles made from it. Soba noodles may be either a mixture of buckwheat and wheat flour, or 100 percent buckwheat flour, the latter being stronger in flavour, and healthier. Cook for 6-7 minutes in plenty of boiling water.

**Chasoba** soba noodles flavoured and coloured with green tea powder. Cook as for regular soba noodles, mixed with them if desired.

# noodles

**Thin udon noodles** made from wheat, these dried noodles should be cooked for 6-8 minutes or until al dente.

Japanese noodles originated in China, but have been a staple part of the Japanese diet for centuries. In Europe they were known first and foremost from their use in Asian stir-fry dishes, but they are now seen as a great alternative to pasta and have become very popular. In fact good pasta can be used as a substitute for Japanese wheat noodles. Ramen (Chinese-style wheat noodles) will also work with most of the recipes in this chapter, as will rice vermicelli. When it comes to gauging quality, noodles are very similar to pasta; the mid-range and organic brands tend to have a better flavour than cheaper lines. Noodles sold in health food stores are often of superior quality. I prefer noodles cooked al dente (tender with some bite remaining) in a pot of salty boiling water and, once done, like to give them a good rinse in cold water for extra shine, before heating them through in the soup or sauce with which they are to be served. If keeping cooked noodles in the fridge I always dress them in a little olive oil to ensure they do not stick together.

**Somen noodles** thin wheat noodles that only need 2 minutes cooking.

**Thick udon noodles** these are precooked and therefore very easy to prepare. They need only a couple of minutes boiling.

# char-grilled baby squid, french beans and quails' eggs in somen soup

serves ● ● ● ●

There is something really bizarre about baby squid. The preparation is like a mini horror film, however it is easy to do, and they have a much tastier texture than their parents. Buy baby squid fresh: the frozen version is very expensive and less tender.

16 baby squid, with tentacles

300g french beans, trimmed

300g dried somen noodles

8 quails' eggs

100ml Simple Teriyaki Sauce (see page 44)

4 tablespoons dashi powder

100ml olive oil

salt and pepper

2 teaspoons bonito flakes

Clean the squid in cold running water and remove the hard membrane from the bodies – this looks like a piece of plastic. Remove any soft tissue using your index finger. Cut between the eyes and tentacles, discarding the eyes and any slimy bits. Rinse in cold water, pat dry and set aside.

Bring a pot of salted water to the boil, add the beans and cook for 2 minutes. Remove the beans using tongs and plunge into ice-cold water. Drain and set aside. Cook the noodles in the same pot of boiling water for 2 minutes, then drain, rinse, and leave to rest in a colander.

Bring a small pan of salted water to the boil. Carefully lower the quails' eggs into the water and cook for 2 minutes. Drain and cool under the tap. Peel the eggs, cut in half, then set aside.

To make the soup, combine the teriyaki sauce, dashi and 1.5 litres of boiling water in a large saucepan or wok and bring to the boil. Add the noodles and reheat gently.

Meanwhile, divide the oil between two bowls and season each batch with salt and pepper. Add the squid to one and the beans to the other and turn gently to coat. Heat a griddle pan and, when it is smoking hot, cook the squid and beans until crisp and slightly charred.

To assemble the dish, divide the noodles and soup among four large bowls. Add the quails' eggs, squid and beans, and finally garnish with a small pinch of bonito flakes.

# japanese style red curry with somen
serves ● ● ● ●

Supermarkets and Asian stores carry most of the ingredients for this dish. The Japanese version of red curry paste is simple to make, however you could substitute an authentic Thai brand. It's not worth trying to make a small quantity, so the recipe here gives about 200ml of curry paste, which will keep in a sterilised jar in the fridge for three months.

200g fresh shitake mushroom

200g mooli, about 15-20cm long

200g baby aubergines

200g butternut squash

200g okra

2 tablespoons vegetable oil

3 heaped tablespoons 'Japanese' Red Curry Paste (see below)

400g can coconut milk

50g creamed coconut block

4 kafir lime leaves

1 stalk lemon grass

2 teaspoons Thai fish sauce

300g dried somen noodles

a small bunch of coriander

**for the 'japanese' red curry paste**

3 small shallots

50g fresh ginger

3 large cloves garlic

3 red chillies

1 stalk lemon grass, or the grated zest of $1/2$ a lemon

1 tablespoon dashi powder

1 tablespoon kimchee base

1 tablespoon cumin

1 tablespoon paprika

50ml extra virgin olive oil

To make the Japanese red curry paste: peel the shallots, ginger and garlic, deseed chillies and chop them all finely. Remove the outer layer of the lemon grass and cut the stalk into thin rings. Combine all these ingredients, plus the dashi, kimchee base, cumin and paprika, in a large mortar or food processor. Start grinding the ingredients to a thick paste, adding the oil gradually. Set aside.

Brush the shitake clean then slice them, leaving the stalks on. Peel the mooli and cut into 5cm-long julienne. Cut the baby aubergines into quarters, leaving the stalks on. Halve the butternut squash lengthways and scrape out the seeds and pith. Cut lengthways again to give four pieces, then cut into $1/2$ cm slices. Trim the okra if necessary.

Heat the wok, add the vegetable oil and, when hot, fry the curry paste for a few minutes to enhance the flavours. Mix in the coconut milk, creamed coconut and 1 litre of boiling water. Add all the vegetables, plus the kafir lime leaves, lemon grass, and fish sauce and simmer for 10 minutes.

Meanwhile, in a large pan of boiling water, cook the somen for 2 minutes. Drain, then rinse in cold water and divide among four large noodle bowls. Ladle the red vegetable curry over the noodles and serve garnished with coriander.

Tip: for a special dinner party version of this dish, add 500g of raw, deveined tiger prawns at the same time you add the vegetables. Leave the tails on for colour and flavour.

# wakame coriander sauce, pancetta and soba

serves ● ● ● ●

Wakame sauce is based on tofu and absolutely fantastic! It is versatile beyond belief and can be served with almost any spuds, pasta, noodles or meats. The super-healthy way to serve it is with brown rice or mooli salad if you are detoxing or dieting; tofu is a perfect source of vegetable protein. However in this recipe I have added a little naughtiness in the form of a good Italian pancetta.

300g chasoba (green tea soba noodles), or a mixture of 150g chasoba and 150g soba noodles

2 tablespoons vegetable oil

200g pancetta, finely diced

**for the wakame sauce**

20g dried wakame seaweed

120g coriander sprigs

1/2 bunch spring onions, roughly chopped

1 large clove garlic, peeled

20g pickled ginger, or fresh ginger, peeled

200g firm tofu

40ml olive oil

4 teaspoons soy sauce

4 teaspoons sesame oil

1 tablespoon runny honey

1 tablespoon dashi powder

salt and pepper

To make the wakame sauce: put the seaweed in a small bowl, cover with cold water and set aside to rehydrate.

Place the coriander in a food processor with the spring onions, garlic and ginger. Break the tofu into chunks and add to the machine. In a small measuring jug combine the olive oil, soy sauce, sesame oil, honey and dashi with 40ml of boiling water. Switch on the food processor and gradually add the liquid, blending until the sauce has the consistency of thick mayonnaise. Transfer the sauce to a mixing bowl. Drain the wakame, stir it into the sauce, and season to taste with salt and pepper.

Bring a pot of boiling salted water to the boil and cook the noodles for 6-7 minutes until they are tender but still have some bite. Drain the noodles in a colander.

Meanwhile, heat 1 tablespoon of vegetable oil in wok and cook the pancetta gently until light golden and just crisp. Transfer to a piece of kitchen paper for a few minutes to absorb the excess fat, and discard the oil in the wok.

Return the wok to a medium heat and add 1 tablespoon of fresh oil. Add the cooked noodles, pancetta and, finally, the wakame sauce, stirring constantly until the ingredients are hot through. Serve immediately.

# spaghetti with chilli jam, cashews and peppers

serves ● ● ● ●

Chilli jam takes several hours to cook, however it is a very therapeutic process and perfect for rainy Sundays when you are pottering around at home. This versatile flavouring brings instant depth to many dishes, from pasta, rice and noodles to fish and poultry. The recipe is derived from one in Australian chef Christine Manfield's excellent book Stir.

300g dried spaghetti

a splash of olive oil

1 large red onion, thinly sliced

2 heaped tablespoons chilli jam

100g raw cashew nuts

2 large red peppers, deseeded and thinly sliced

50g rocket leaves

salt and pepper

**for the chilli jam**

350g large red chillies, roughly chopped

100g birds' eye chillies, roughly chopped

2 large brown onions, roughly chopped

4 cloves garlic, roughly chopped

250ml sunflower, grapeseed or vegetable oil

20g tamarind paste

35g palm sugar

Make the chilli jam at least one day in advance. Combine the chillies, onions and garlic in a food processor and blend, gradually adding the oil to make a paste. Pour into a wide, heavy-based saucepan and cook gently over a low heat for 6-7 hours, or until the paste is thick and dark red, stirring every half hour to prevent sticking or burning.

Meanwhile, in a small bowl, steep the tamarind paste in 75ml hot water. Use a teaspoon to break up the paste as much as possible then set aside for 20 minutes, stirring occasionally. Sieve the mixture to give 75ml of tamarind liquid. Dissolve the palm sugar (grate it first if necessary) in the tamarind then, when the chill paste is thick and dark red, add the tamarind mixture to the pan and continue cooking for a further hour or so, stirring occasionally. Leave the chilli jam to cool down, then store in a sterilised jar in the fridge, where it will keep for up to 3 months.

Bring a pot of salted water to the boil and cook the pasta according to the packet instructions. Drain and set aside.

Place a wok over a medium heat. Add a splash of olive oil and fry the onion until soft. Add 2 heaped tablespoons of chilli jam and stir until the onions are well coated. Add the cashews and red peppers and stir-fry for a few minutes. Finally add the cooked spaghetti and rocket and stir until hot through. Season with salt and pepper and serve.

# wild mushroom ragout with udon and shaved parmesan

serves ● ● ● ●

The shitake mushroom is one of the undisputed heroes of Japanese cuisine, adding flavour and texture to almost any dish. Both dried and fresh shitake are now widely available in the West. The dried version needs to be reconstituted in water; fresh shitake cost a few pennies more, but are worth it for the taste. In this recipe you can use any wild mushrooms available locally, such as pied a mouton, oyster, morel, pied bleu, or trompette de la mort, to name a few. Mushrooms are a sensitive bunch, so the best way to clean them is to brush gently with a pastry brush. However, first cut off the dirty ends, leaving as much of the stalks on as possible as these are full of flavour.

300g flat dried udon noodles
100g parmesan cheese, cut into flakes

**for the mushroom ragout**
2 tablespoons olive oil
1 large onion, finely chopped
200g mixed wild mushrooms, roughly chopped
200g brown chestnut mushrooms, quartered
100g fresh shitake mushrooms, thinly sliced
125ml mirin
125ml sake
2-3 tablespoons cornflour
100g curly parsley sprigs, finely chopped
50g chives, roughly chopped
salt and pepper

To make the ragout: heat the olive oil in a wok and fry the chopped onion until golden. Add the prepared mushrooms and turn them gently in the oil, cooking for 8 minutes. Add the mirin and sake, cover with a lid and leave to simmer over a gentle heat for 20 minutes, stirring occasionally.

Meanwhile, cook the udon in a pot of boiling salted water for 7-8 minutes until al dente, or just cooked. Drain the noodles in a colander.

Dissolve the cornflour in 200ml of cold water. Add the slaked cornflour gradually to the mushroom ragout until it thickens – you may not need it all. Stir in the fresh herbs and season to taste with salt and pepper.

Remove half the ragout from the wok and set aside in a bowl. Add the noodles to the wok and turn them in the ragout until they have heated through. Divide the noodles among four large bowls, top with the remaining ragout and plenty of parmesan cheese.

# moroccan pumpkin ragout with soba noodle soup

serves • • • •

This recipe is Japan-meets-North-Africa, which admittedly sounds like a very odd fusion of ingredients. Nonetheless it is the best comfort food for those first winter days, when I realise that hibernation is again upon us and I long for energy-giving food. The ragout tastes better after a few days in the fridge, so it's a good idea to make a double portion.

800g pumpkin

1 tablespoon cumin powder

1 tablespoon coriander powder

$1/2$ tablespoon shichimi or other chilli powder

$1/2$ tablespoon garam masala

100ml olive oil

2 shallots, finely chopped

2 cloves garlic, finely chopped

500ml tomato juice

70g sultanas

70g pine nuts

1 stick cinnamon

salt and pepper

300g dried soba noodles

4 tablespoons dashi powder

100ml Simple Teriyaki Sauce (see page 44)

Peel, deseed and cube the pumpkin.

Toast the cumin, coriander, shichimi and garam masala in a dry frying pan over a low heat until fragrant. Immediately transfer to a small dish and set aside.

Working in two batches, heat half the olive oil in a large wok over medium heat. Add half the shallots and garlic and fry until softened. Add half the toasted spices and half the pumpkin and fry for another 5 minutes, stirring to coat the pumpkin with the spice mixture. Transfer the mixture to a large pot and repeat with the remaining olive oil, shallots, garlic, spices and pumpkin.

Add the tomato juice and 200ml cold water to the pot, then mix in the sultanas, pine nuts, cinnamon stick and some salt. Cover and simmer for up to $1^{1}/2$ hours, stirring every 15 minutes. When all the liquid has evaporated and the mixture is a rich dark colour, the ragout is ready. Season to taste with salt and pepper.

Shortly before the ragout is finished cooking, bring a pot of salted water to the boil and cook the soba noodles for 6-7 minutes until al dente, or just cooked. Meanwhile, make the soup: combine the dashi powder, teriyaki sauce and 1.5 litres of boiling water in a saucepan and bring to the boil.

When the noodles are ready, drain them and divide among four large noodle bowls. Carefully pour the soup over each portion and top with the ragout before serving.

# udon moules marinière with baby plum tomatoes and fresh herbs

serves ● ● ● ●

Moules Marinière is one of the best-recognised shellfish dishes in the world and surely deserves this Japanese interpretation.

1.5kg mussels

600g frozen chunky udon noodles

2 tablespoons olive oil

2 shallots, finely chopped

2 garlic cloves, finely chopped

100g flat-leaf parsley sprigs,
    finely chopped

175ml dry white wine

2 tablespoons dashi powder

200g baby plum tomatoes, halved

50ml double cream

salt and pepper

50g basil leaves, torn

Scrub the mussels using a scouring pad and plenty of cold water. Pull off any beards. Tap any open mussels sharply – if they do not close they are dead and should be discarded.

Place the frozen udon noodles in large bowl and cover with cold water. Put a large kettle of water on to boil.

Heat the olive oil in a large saucepan and gently fry the shallots and garlic until light golden. Stir in the parsley, then add 300ml of boiling water from the kettle, and the white wine. Put the cleaned mussels in the saucepan, cover and cook for 3-4 minutes, shaking the pan occasionally to ensure that they cook evenly. The mussels are done when they are all open. Using a slotted spoon, remove them to a plate and set aside.

Add 1 litre of boiling water to the cooking juices in the pan, then stir in the dashi powder and halved tomatoes. Cook for a few minutes, then stir in the cream and season to taste with salt and pepper.

Divide the udon noodles among four large bowls. Ladle the soup over the noodles, top with the mussels and garnish with torn basil leaves. The dish is ready to serve.

# teriyaki salmon with warm soba salad

serves • • • •

This is a Feng classic – my best-selling special of all time. After seven years I am tempted to take it off the menu, but staff have threatened me with strike action, so fond are they of this dish. It is fast, simple and tasty. For this recipe I use Loch Duart salmon which not only is heavenly raw, but also cooks perfectly. Ask for the salmon skin to be left on. You will need about half a side for four people. As you can see from the picture, I like to cut it differently from the traditional way of presenting salmon steak. To do this, halve the side lengthways along the line of the spine, then cut each piece diagonally into portions.

300g soba noodles, or a mixture of
    150g soba and 150g chasoba
    (green tea soba noodles)
olive oil, for frying
4 salmon fillets, about 140g each
1 large red onion, finely chopped
2 garlic cloves, finely chopped
100g pine nuts
100g rocket leaves

**to serve**
200ml Simple Teriyaki Sauce
    (see page 44)

First prepare the teriyaki sauce according to the method on page 44. Preheat the oven to 180°C/Gas 4. Bring a large pan of salted water to the boil. Cook both varieties of soba togther until al dente (or tender but with some bite remaining) then drain and set aside in a colander.

To cook the salmon: pour a good splash of olive oil into a large frying pan and place over a high heat. Place the fillets in the oil skin-side down and fry for 2-3 minutes. Season with salt and pepper, then turn the fillets over and season again. Continue cooking for another 2-3 minutes. Transfer the salmon to a baking tray and place in the oven for 6-8 minutes, or until the salmon is just cooked through.

Pour a little olive oil into a wok and fry the onion and garlic until golden. Add the pine nuts, rocket and cooked soba noodles and stir until all the ingredients are hot through.

Divide the noodle mixture among four large plates and place the cooked salmon carefully on top. Drizzle each portion with the teriyaki sauce before serving.

First wash the rice following the instructions on page 15, then leave in the sieve to dry for 30 minutes.

Meanwhile, make a half quantity of the tempura batter as per the recipe on page 118 and place in the fridge to rest. Clean the baby squid (see page 146) and place in the fridge.

Put a kettle of water on to boil. Place the dashi powder in a large jug and cover with 1 litre of boiling water from the kettle, stirring to dissolve.

Heat the olive oil in a wok and fry the shallots, garlic, shitake and pine nuts until golden. Add the sushi rice and cook, stirring, for a few minutes to ensure that all the grains are well coated. Ladle about 100ml of the hot dashi stock into the wok and stir until the liquid has been absorbed. Repeat with another ladle of dashi stock, stirring until it has been absorbed. Continue this process of adding stock and stirring until the rice is cooked but the grains still have a little bite.

Add the teriyaki sauce and plum wine and stir until absorbed. Season to taste with salt and pepper, then cover, remove from the heat and set aside in a warm place.

To prepare the baby squid tempura: heat the vegetable oil to 180°C in a large heavy-based saucepan or electric deep-fryer. Meanwhile, cut the body of each squid into 3 pieces, so that you have chunky rings. Turn rings and the tentacles in a bowl of tempura flour, then dip in the prepared batter and fry for 1-2 minutes, or until golden. Drain the squid on kitchen paper and season with salt.

Divide the risotto among four shallow serving bowls and top with the rocket leaves and grated parmesan. Serve with a dish of the baby squid tempura on the side.

300g raw sushi rice
2 tablespoons dashi powder
2 tablespoons olive oil
2 shallots, chopped
2 garlic cloves, chopped
6 fresh shitake mushrooms, finely chopped
50g pine nuts
50ml Simple Teriyaki Sauce (see page 44)
50ml plum wine
salt and pepper
50g rocket leaves
50g parmesan cheese, coarsely grated

**for the baby squid tempura**
500ml Tempura Batter (see page 118)
8 baby squid
tempura flour, for dusting
2 litres vegetable oil, for deep-frying

# japanese style risotto with baby squid tempura

serves ● ● ● ●

On certain days the low-carb diet
needs to be put aside for old-style soul
food such as this dish, which combines
the best Japanese ingredients and
traditional Italian cooking.

# desserts

Japanese cuisine does not include desserts
as we in the West generally know them.
Maybe it is because the Japanese meal is
so perfect that it does not need a rich, heavy
ending. The standard dessert offered in sushi
bars is a simple scoop of green tea ice cream,
very much an acquired taste but nevertheless
gaining popularity worldwide. Here are my
interpretations of Japanese desserts, all very
grown up in their flavours – strong, savoury,
bitter and sweet. With the exception of the
Rice Krispie Layer Cake, they should
be served in small portions.

Dark chocolate, brazil nut and nori maki with Espressotini

# poached pears with shiso and cream cheese in pink maki

serves • • • •

This dish is perfect for the picnic basket and absolutely divine at brunch with a glass of chilled champagne. I first used 'pink sheet', which is made from soy beans instead of seaweed, when I was casting about for something child-friendly on the menu. The children really liked it; the adults loved it. These make a great light meal for a hot summer's day.

2 ripe pale-skinned pears
5 tablespoons mirin
100ml sake
2 tablespoons caster sugar
4 pieces pink soy bean sheet
500g Prepared Sushi Rice (see page 15)
100g Philadelphia Lite cream cheese
seeds from 2 pomegranates
1 punnet shiso cress

Cut the pears into eighths, put in a saucepan with the mirin, sake and sugar. Bring to the boil, lower the heat and leave to simmer for about 20 minutes. When the pears are cooked through, drain in a sieve and leave to cool.

Using one of the 'pink sheets' in place of nori, trim it by one-fifth and place on a rolling mat as described on pages 88-9. Spread 125g of the sushi rice evenly across the sheet, leaving a border of about 2cm clear along the top. Using a spatula, spread a generous layer of cream cheese across the rice, then add pieces of the poached pear and sprinkle with sprigs of shiso cress.

Holding the filling in place with your index fingers, roll the maki into a neat cylinder and use the clear tab of pink sheet to seal it. Repeat the process with the remaining pink sheets, rice, cream cheese and pear.

Use the sides of the rolling mat to square up the maki and leave each one to rest for a few minutes. Remove from the rolling mat, trim off the rough ends, then cut each roll crossways into three pieces.

Arrange three pieces on each plate, scatter with the pomegranate seeds and garnish with shiso before serving.

# green tea cheesecake

serves ••••
••••

I use ginger biscuits instead of digestives to make the base for this very dense but refreshing cheesecake because their flavour complements the green tea very well.

200g good quality ginger biscuits

60g butter, plus extra for greasing

75ml double cream

3 tablespoons green tea powder (matcha), plus extra for dusting

225g full fat cream cheese

3 tablespoons caster sugar

1 egg

1 egg yolk

200ml crème fraîche

Preheat the oven to 180°C (Gas 4) and butter an 18-20cm diameter spring-form cake tin. Crush the biscuits in a food processor and place in a mixing bowl. Gently melt the butter and add to the biscuit crumbs, mixing well. Press the crumbs into the base of the tin using your knuckles to form a firm layer, then chill for about 10 minutes to help it set. Bake for 10 minutes or until the base is light golden. Remove from the oven and set aside to cool.

Reduce the oven temperature to 150°C (Gas 2). In a small saucepan, heat the double cream gently and mix the green tea powder into it. (Do not let the cream go over 85°C or the mixture will split.) In a large mixing bowl, beat the cream cheese and sugar together. Add the egg and egg yolk, then the green tea mixture.

Pour the cheese mixture over the biscuit base and bake in the lower part of the oven for 30 minutes. Turn off the oven and leave the cheesecake to cool down in the oven for at least an hour before transferring it to the fridge. Serve with the crème fraîche, sprinkled with some additional green tea powder to decorate.

# dark chocolate, brazil nut and nori maki

makes

Dark chocolate and nori is a special combination best enjoyed with a strong coffee or Espressotini (see below) after a satisfying meal. Use top quality chocolate because in this recipe a little goes a long way.

200g good quality 70% dark chocolate
15g unsalted butter
$1/2$ shot espresso, or other strong coffee
100g brazil nuts
1 sheet nori

Fill a small saucepan with water to a depth of about 5cm and place a metal bowl on top. Place over a moderate heat. Break up the chocolate and add to the bowl so that it melts gently. Add the butter and coffee, stirring constantly to ensure a smooth finish. Remove from the heat.

Roughly chop the brazil nuts and add them to the melted chocolate. Leave to rest for 10 minutes to harden a little.

Trim down the nori sheet by one-fifth and place on a rolling mat shiny side down. Place all of the chocolate mixture in the middle and gently roll into a square-sided maki roll (see technique page 88-9). Set the chocolate maki aside in the rolling mat in a cool place to rest for a few hours.

Use a sharp knife to cut the chocolate nori into twelve small pieces and serve as little bites with hot coffee or chilled Espressotini (see recipe below).

# espressotini

makes ● ● ● ●

a handful of ice cubes
8 shots of espresso, of a strong small pot of cafetière coffee
4 shots vodka
4 shots coffee liqueur

Place the ice cubes in a jug or cocktail shaker. Add the coffee, vodka and liqueur and shake well. Pour into tall glasses and serve with the Dark Chocolate, Brazil Nut and Nori Maki (above), Rice Krispie Layer Cake (pages 166-7), or simply as an after-dinner drink in place of dessert.

Make the ice cream one day in advance. Place 500ml of the cream in a saucepan with the yolks and sugar. Split open the vanilla pods, scrape out the seeds, and add to the pan with the pods. Place over a moderate heat and, using an electric whisk, whisk the mixture while heating it to a temperature of 80°C exactly (use a thermometer). Transfer to a plastic container and freeze immediately. When the mixture is solid, cut into large chunks and blend in a food processor until the lumps turn to soft ice. Meanwhile, whip the remaining 500ml cream until stiff. Fold the soft ice into the whipped cream and freeze again for 24 hours or so.

To make the Rice Krispie layer cakes: grease a 40 x 30cm baking tray. Melt the butter in a small saucepan over a medium heat. Add the marshmallows and stir until melted, then mix in the honey. In a large bowl combine the Rice Krispies and sesame seeds. Add the marshmallow mixture and stir until well combined. Pour into the baking tray and spread out evenly with a buttered spoon. Place a piece of greaseproof paper over the top and sit something heavy, such as a phone book, on top. Set aside.

For the coulis: combine the berries, mirin or sake, and sugar in a small saucepan. Add just enough water to cover and simmer over a medium heat for 10 minutes. Sieve the mixture into a bowl, pressing the berries against the mesh of the sieve to extract as much liquid as possible. Return the coulis to the pan and place over a medium heat. In a small bowl, blend the cornflour with a little cold water and gradually stir into the coulis, so that it thickens to the consistency of double cream. Pour the sauce into a squeeze bottle and set aside.

Using a 7cm pastry ring, cut 8 discs from the Rice Krispie cake. Place one on a serving dish, add a scoop of ice cream and drizzle with coulis. Top with another Rice Krispie disc. Repeat with the remaining ingredients, then finish with berries.

30g unsalted butter, plus extra for greasing
150g white marshmallows
2 tablespoons honey
150g Rice Krispies, preferably organic
70g white toasted sesame seeds
a few berries, to decorate

for the ice cream
1 litre whipping cream, preferably organic
8 large egg yolks
150g caster sugar
2 vanilla pods

for the fruit coulis
100g raspberries
100g blackberries
50ml mirin or sake
50g caster sugar
1-2 tablespoons cornflour

# rice krispie layer cake with fynen vanilla ice cream

This dessert is my tribute to my mother's amazing Fynen vanilla ice cream, for which she always uses top quality vanilla pods. Fynen is the island in Denmark where I grew up and is well known for its dairy products. The recipe here makes 1 litre so there is plenty left over for other treats. I've combined it with a layer cake – another Fynen speciality – made of soft biscuits of sesame, marshmallow and Rice Krispies.

serves ● ● ● ●

# black sesame and maple syrup ice cream

serves ● ● ● ● ● ● ●

If you serve this ice cream once it will be expected again and again, and you'll find guests won't go home without it! It makes heavenly, happy 'afters' served with a small, strong cup of espresso made from the very best, freshly ground beans. I find one large scoop tends to suffice as it it's so dense with seeds and flavour that any more would be gluttonous.

150ml organic cream
250ml full fat organic milk
60ml organic maple syrup
4 egg yolks
50g caster sugar
100g toasted black sesame seeds

Combine the cream, milk and maple syrup in a saucepan and heat the mixture to just under boiling point.

In a large mixing bowl, whisk together the egg yolks and sugar. Slowly pour the hot milk mixture over the egg yolks, whisking continually, then return the custard mixture to the saucepan. Heat very slowly and carefully, stirring constantly to ensure the mixture does not curdle.

When it reaches 74°C exactly, transfer the mixture to a jug and leave to cool. Once it has reached room temperature, place the jug in the refrigerator to chill thoroughly.

Use a mortar and pestle, or the small bowl of a food processor, to grind half the sesame seeds. Add them, plus the remaining whole sesame seeds, to the cold custard and pour into an ice cream machine.

Churn the mixture until almost frozen, then transfer it to a plastic container and freeze until solid. If you don't have an ice cream maker, pour the mixture straight into the plastic container and place in the freezer, giving it a stir every 30 minutes or so until frozen.

Once made the ice cream keeps for up to a month (like it is going to last that long...). To serve, simply place a large scoop in a beautiful bowl.

# japanese ingredients used in this book

**Dashi** a stock made of shavings of dried bonito, a fish of the tuna family. Dashi has natural flavour enhancing properties and is the base of much Japanese cooking, from sauces and soups to noodles.

**Edamame** young green soy beans. These are typically served in the pod, with sea salt or mirin dipping sauce, as an appetizer or snack. However you will often find them podded and used in salads.

**Ginger, pickled** known as gari in Japanese, pickled ginger is served with sushi and sashimi to cleanse the palate between different flavours. It can also be used as an ingredient in sauces and salads.

**Kimchee base** kimchee are Korean pickled vegetables traditionally served with every meal,. Kimchee base is a bright red, ready-made product popular in Japan as a convenient way to make pickled vegetables. It looks much like a spicy tomato sauce but is made of garlic, chilli, ginger, vinegar and salt. Also suitable as a sauce for dipping, in this book it is often used as a flavouring ingredient too.

**Kombu** also known as kelp, this variety of seaweed is used as a flavour enhancer in sauces, marinades and sushi vinegar.

**Mirin** sweet cooking sake, also used in marinades, sauces and tamago (Japanese omelette).

**Miso paste** a fermented paste of soy beans, sometimes with barley or rice, and salt. It is used in soups, salad dressings and marinades. The fermented soy protein tenderises meat or fish after 2-3 days of marinating. Miso is very nutritious, high in protein (14 per cent) and comes in white, red and dark brown varieties. White miso is the softest and mildest, red miso is rounder in its flavour, while the dark variety is rich and deeply flavoured. Miso paste is often mixed with sugar, mirin and sake to provide extra flavour and to give dishes a caramelised finish.

**Mizuna** this salad leaf originated in Japan but is now also grown in Italy. Mizuna has a crisp, peppery taste, like mild rocket leaves.

**Mooli** often called daikon or Chinese radish, this large white radish is integral to Japanese cuisine as an aid for digestion. Finely grated mooli is always served with raw fish and tempura to help the body digest the fatty components, however it is becoming more common in salads. Be sure to grate it very finely in long shreds.

**Nori** sheets of pressed seaweed, mostly kelp. Toasted nori is used for making maki and temaki sushi. Very high in iodine, fibre and totally non-fat, like all seaweed it can be categorised as a superfood. Nori flakes are also sold for sprinkling over food as a seasoning.

**Ponzu sauce** a mix of evaporated sake. soy sauce and the juice of ponzu, which is a fragrant Japanese citrus fruit. Typically served as a dipping sauce, it can also be used as a marinade and an ingredient in modern desserts.

**Rice vinegar** vinegar made from rice. It is the main ingredient of sushi vinegar, but also used in marinades and dressings. Vinegar has an important position in Japanese cuisine and is considered a body cleanser so is often used in soft drinks and natural health products.

**Sesame oil** is extracted from sesame seeds. It has a strong, distinctive flavour and a very high burning point. Sesame oil is often mixed with corn or vegetable oil for frying tempura and is a frequent inclusion in dressings and marinades. Remember sesame is categorised as a nut and anyone suffering from nut allergies may have a reaction to it.

**Sesame seeds** available in white and black varieties, these are served toasted as a topping for vegetables and rice, and are also frequently used in sushi.

**Shichimi** Japanese seven-spice chilli powder. Traditionally served as a table condiment with noodles, it can also be used to give a spicy kick to sushi rolls.

**Shiso** in Japan large shiso leaves are traditionally served with sashimi and temaki, however as they are at present only imported to Europe by airfreight, I prefer to use the smaller shiso cress, punnets of which come from Holland by road and sea. Shiso cress looks like mini basil leaves and has an aniseed flavour and fragrance reminiscent of Thai basil. It is perfect with everything, including desserts.

**Shitake mushrooms** the best known of the Japanese fungi. They are often sold dried, to be reconstituted in hot water, however fresh shitake mushrooms are now widely available as they are grown all over Europe, including Britain, and the fresh mushroom is much preferred.

**Soba noodles** buckwheat noodles. Can be made from a mixture of wheat and buckwheat, or with 100 percent buckwheat, the later being the healthiest option. Buckwheat is a complex carbohydrate and good for the metabolism. Soba is used in soups, salads as well as noodle dishes.

**Somen noodles** very thin wheat noodles most commonly used in soup noodle dishes.

**Soy sauce**  the grandfather of Japanese ingredients, served with or used in almost all Japanese cuisine. It is brewed from soy beans and wheat, and has a low alcohol content of two percent. I prefer to use the soy sauce brewed in Europe under licence to Kikkoman (Japan's leading manufacturer) because imported soy arrives by sea and suffers when crossing the Equator: the alcohol evaporates in the heat, making the soy sauce thick and a little bitter. Soy sauce is seen as the salt of Asian cuisine, and dishes seasoned with soy sauce should not need additional salt.

**Sushi vinegar** I prefer using ready-mixed sushi vinegar as it ensures consistency throughout our restaurants. My preferred brand is Mitsukan, but you can certainly mix your own: gently heat 60ml rice vinegar with 100g caster sugar, 2 teaspoons salt and a 10cm piece kombu seaweed. When the sugar has dissolved, leave the mixture to cool down to room temperature and remove the kombu.

**Tempura flour** often called tempura-ko, this specialist flour is made of wheat and corn flour. It has a very light texture and is essential for light, crisp tempura.

**Teriyaki sauce** a thick sauce used with grilled fish or meat. It can be bought ready made, but is easy to make yourself (see page 44).

**Tobiko** flying fish roe, often flavoured with yuzu, wasabi or ume (plum), available in Japanese stores. Masago is a cheaper alternative: the eggs are smaller and often artificially coloured.

**Tofu** also known as bean curd, tofu is made of soy beans and very high in protein. It is highly versatile and can be eaten raw, fried, steamed, braised, or puréed to give a base for sauces such as the wakame sauce on page 149.

**Udon** thick wheat noodles popular at street food stalls in Tokyo.

**Wakame** a type of seaweed sold dried and reconstituted in cold water before use. Wakame is high in iodine and fibre and a good inclusion in soups and salads.

**Wasabi** Japanese horseradish. Traditionally found growing wild by rivers on mountainsides, it is now cultivated on the banks of streams. The fresh root is grated and served as a condiment for sashimi and sushi. Wasabi powder should be mixed to a thick paste with cold water. Ready-made wasabi pastes are also readily available.

**Wasabi peas** spicy snacks made from dried peas coated with a strong, wasabi flavoured crust. Traditionally eaten as a snack, they are excellent crushed and used as an ingredient in sushi.

**Yuzu juice** juice made from the yuzu, a Japanese citrus fruit with a fragrant aroma. It is an excellent ingredient for dressings and marinades. If not available, yuzu juice can be replaced with freshly squeezed grapefruit.

# where to buy japanese ingredients

Shopping for Japanese ingredients has become much easier over the last decade as the cuisine has gained in popularity. Basic ingredients for making sushi – rice, sushi vinegar, nori, wasabi, pickled ginger and soy sauce – are widely available in larger supermarkets, food halls, and health food stores. Other ingredients commonly used in Japanese cooking, such as sesame seeds, mirin, sesame oil, fresh shitake mushroom and mooli, are also readily available in the above places, and all the other vegetables used in this book can be purchased from good greengrocers or large supermarkets. However, when it comes to raw fish, I must emphasise that supermarket fish is not sushi-grade. Instead use a good local fishmonger with a fine reputation and remind the person behind the counter that you are going to be serving the fish raw in sushi and sashimi.

For more specialised Japanese ingredients such as shichimi, tempura flour and wasabi peas, there are quite a few places in London and other cities with an excellent choice of imported products. When shopping at Asian stores that offer a broad range, I always recommend going for the mid-priced lines as these are good quality yet reasonably priced. I believe you have to be a serious connoisseur to go for the most expensive products, an extra spend I do not bother with as I would not be able to tell the difference. Note that very often Thai, Chinese and other specialist Asian stores carry Japanese products too.

Below are some of my favourite shops, plus a few other recommendations.

**The Japan Centre**
212 Piccadilly, London W1 (020 7434 4218) www.japancentre.com

**Oriental City**
399 Edgware Road, Colindale, London NW9 (020-8200-0009)

**Atari-Ya Foods**
7 Station Parade, Noel Road, London W3 (020 8896 1552) www.atariya.co.uk
Branches at 595 High Road, London N12 (020 8446 6669)and 15-16 Monkville Parade, Finchley Road, London NW11 (020 8458 7626).

**Lotte Shopping**
26 Malden Road, New Malden, Surrey (020 8942 9552).

**Miura Foods**
44 Coombe Road, Kingston, Surrey (020 8549 8079) www.miurafoods.com
Branch at 5 Limpsfield Road, Sanderstead, South Croydon (020 8651 4498).

**Jasmin Food Shop**
Stanton House Hotel, The Avenue, Stanton Fitzwarren, Swindon, Wiltshire (01793 861 777) www.stantonhouse.co.uk

**Mai Bai's**
4 Bamford Road, Didsbury , Manchester (07795 160272)

**Oki-Nami**
12 York Place, Brighton, East Sussex (01273 677 702) www.okinami.com

**Midori**
19 Marlborough Place, Brighton, East Sussex (01273 601 460)

**Setsu Japan**
196a Heaton Road, Newcastle upon Tyne (0191 265 9970)

**Akaneya**
81 Northumberland Avenue, Reading (0118 931 0448)

## For online shopping

**Mount Fuji** (01743 741169)
www.mountfuji.co.uk
**Goodness Direct** (0871 871 6611)
www.goodnessdirect.co.uk

## Australia and New Zealand

**Tokyo Mart**
27 Northbridge Plaza, Sailors Bay Road, Northbridge, NSW (02 9958 6860)

**Fuji Mart**
34A Elizabeth Street, South Yarra, Victoria (03 9826 5839)

**Fuji Mart**
Shop 1, Southport Park Shopping Centre, cnr Ferry and Benowa Roads, Southport, Queensland (07 5591 6211)

**Made in Nippon**
313 Queen Street, Auckland, New Zealand (09 377 1891)

# index

Entries in **bold** indicate photographs.

## acknowledgements

First I would like to thank my business partner Jeremy
Rose for supporting me, believing in my abilities as a chef
and helping to get this book published. Feng Sushi has
provided me with a framework to develop and try new and
interesting things, therefore I also would like to thank
Chris McFadden our financial backer for his support and
active role with Feng Sushi. The staff at Feng Sushi – in
particular the excellent team of head chefs I work with on
a daily basis – are all to thank for the success Feng Sushi
has become. Without their hard work we would never be
where we are today. Thanks to all of Feng Sushi's main
suppliers: Tazaki Food, Aberdeen Sea Products and
Leanards for their lovely produce. I would also like to
thank Tanis Taylor who helped with the original pitch for
this book. Special thanks to Lars, and all the talented
people at Quadrille, for working so hard on this book.
Finally thank you to my fiancé David for his support,
brutally honest criticism and always cooking and serving
me a lovely meal at the end of a long day.

This paperback edition first published in 2007 by
Quadrille Publishing Limited
Alhambra House
27-31 Charing Cross Road
London WC2H 0LS

Text © 2006 Silla Bjerrum
Photographs © 2006 Lars Ranek
Design and layout © 2006 Quadrille Publishing Ltd

**Editorial director** Anne Furniss
**Creative director** Helen Lewis
**Project editor** Jenni Muir
**Photographer** Lars Ranek
**Food styling** Silla Bjerrum
**Designer** Claire Peters
**Production** Ruth Deary

The rights of the authors have been asserted.
All rights reserved. No part of this book may be
reproduced, stored in a retrieval system or transmitted
in any form or by any means, electronic, electrostatic,
magnetic tape, mechanical, photocopying, recording
or otherwise, without the prior permission in writing of
the publisher.
Although all reasonable care has been taken in the
preparation of this book, neither the publisher, editors
nor the authors can accept any liability for any
consequences arising from the use thereof, or the
information contained therein.

Cataloguing in Publication Data: a catalogue record for this
book is available from the British Library.

ISBN:978 184400 496 6

Printed and bound in China